Fundraising Is...

Fundraising Is...
Everything Done
Before Asking
for Money

Patrick Belcher

NEW YORK

LONDON • NASHVILLE • MELBOURNE • VANCOUVER

Fundraising Is...
Everything Done Before Asking for Money

Published in New York, New York, by Morgan James Publishing. Morgan James is a trademark of Morgan James, LLC. www.MorganJamesPublishing.com

Morgan James BOGO™

A **FREE** ebook edition is available for you or a friend with the purchase of this print book.

CLEARLY SIGN YOUR NAME ABOVE

Instructions to claim your free ebook edition:
1. Visit MorganJamesBOGO.com
2. Sign your name CLEARLY in the space above
3. Complete the form and submit a photo of this entire page
4. You or your friend can download the ebook to your preferred device

ISBN 978-1-63195-407-8 paperback
ISBN 978-1-63195-408-5 eBook
Library of Congress Control Number:
2020922213

Cover Design by:
Rachel Lopez
www.r2cdesign.com

Morgan James is a proud partner of Habitat for Humanity Peninsula and Greater Williamsburg. Partners in building since 2006.

Get involved today! Visit
MorganJamesPublishing.com/giving-back

This book is dedicated to my parents who taught us that the greatest gift you can ever give is one's time and talent.

And to my son who motivates me everyday to be the best version of myself.

Contents

Acknowledgments

This may be the toughest part of the whole book to write. I have been very fortunate in my life to be introduced to many amazing people that have contributed in some meaningful way to who I am and what made this book possible. As I write this, my head is spinning with the names of so many, so please forgive me if I forget to mention you.

I must begin with my parents, Katie and Richard, who spent their lives not only teaching me but also illustrating the value of relationships. The attendance at their funerals was a great testament to this.

To Heath Rada, who first planted the seed of being a professional fundraiser in my head. The ground may have seemed impenetrable; however, it just took a little while for that seed to take root. Thanks to Heather Livingston who helped me to realize the value of my years of sales training as it applied to fundraising. You helped to fertilize and grow that seed and helped me to cultivate my experience into this book.

To Rocky Russell and Julie Dudley, my first official clients that found value in my strategic solutions, which, fortunately, yielded some real results. To all my clients who inspire many of my blogs and helped me develop the strategies included in these pages. Also, thank you to my many peers at Association of Fundraising Professionals-Hampton Roads and Network Peninsula that have contributed in many ways to my knowledge.

To Chris Jones, coach, friend, and taskmaster. Without you, this book still would be just a random collection of blogs. And thank you to Morgan James Publishing for taking my book to the world.

No person is an island. My family is extremely important to me. To my son Jacob, because of you I strive to always be the best and someone you can always be proud of calling Dad. To my brother Chris and his family that have always been proud of PB&J marComm and considered me the cool uncle. Especially my sister-n-law, Leah, who helped edit this book and kept me aware that everyone does not view fundraising as something "fun," as I do. To Elizabeth "Libby" Westley who has been a muse, partner, editor, confidante, and best friend, one who has been a part of every step of this book and my development as an entrepreneur. Thank you all for your love, confidence, and support.

Books have no value without you the reader. Thank you for picking up this book and believing in the promise that I want to help you be a better fundraiser. You are truly appreciated.

CHAPTER 1

CLIMBING A MOUNTAIN

Congrats on being an integral part of the world of non-profits. You are a game-changer in your community. Great fundraisers value people, make a difference, and hypnotize people with their storytelling. The choice to become a professional fundraiser is every bit as challenging and rewarding as choosing to climb a mountain.

Ed Barnard, a blogger on the *Visit Rainier* website calls his first ascent on Mount Rainier the adventure of a lifetime. Furthermore, he talks about how special the experience was.

Barnard's blog could easily be talking about the world of fundraising as much as climbing a mountain when he shares, "It's often a fast pace. At the least, it will *feel* fast because so much is happening at once." In climbing, there is your pack, the weather, your footing, physical condition, mental preparation, lighting, and the people climbing with you. In fundraising, there are campaigns, events, stewardship, cultivation, social media, storytelling, and then all the relationships one must leverage. As Barnard explains, in preparation for his climb, there is both physical conditioning and technical skills. A fundraiser can discuss the multiple tasks that are necessary and that require personal stamina and mental discipline of a solid strategy. He shares there are many good books about Rainier, and you should educate yourself, but a successful climb requires connecting with an experienced climber.

Please allow this book to serve as one of your guides and resource. *Fundraising Is: Everything Done Before Asking For Money* will be better when it is discussed and shared with an experienced colleague. Through discussion, you and your colleagues will grow. As the author, it was through this connection with someone of experience that I realized the value of my training in sales, and she helped me connect the dots. The new guy was helping a twenty-five-plus-year fundraising veteran sharpen her skills, and she helped me to understand my potential.

Barnard talks passionately about how preparation begins by getting to know the surroundings. It is important to "understand" the mountain. You must understand the different routes to the top, the vegetation, the wildlife, and the weather. In his blog, he observes the vegetation and wildlife and where the water was and what approaches had more access to water and the sun. In fundraising, it is no different. Certain approaches raise more money than others, or donors (like wildlife) respond to activity in their ecosystems in different ways. Barnard shares that there will be multiple groups on the same approach and some will pass you, and at times, your group will pass others. Notice them and acknowledge them, but it is not necessary to compete with them. There are multiple reasons for the different pace. The same in fundraising, many groups will try the same approach with varying results. This may be their twentieth time while this is only your first. Their needs may be different, so they must move faster. Don't compete; just be aware.

Aptly, he shares that getting ready to climb Mount Rainier requires the "3 Ps: preparation, planning, and practice." He talks about how there are different ways to kick it up a notch with different gear, like the latest equipment and GPS and cell phone technology. One of the most interesting activities he shares is about hiking at night with out a flashlight to practice and become familiar with the environment of darkness. After all, one of the best times to hike is before the sun comes up and you may not have the hand for a particular flashlight or want to ensure a headlamp comfortably fits on your gear.

Fundraising requires the same "3 *P*s." There are often ways you step up your fundraising through added software or new activities. However, sometimes you just need to experience the terrain or the activity. This could be putting on your own campaign or attending and helping with other organization's campaigns. And sometimes, as much as you would like, you don't have an extra hand or have the ability to comfortably fit in one more component. For instance, as simple and easy as it seems a raffle is to organize, there is no room at your event.

Subsequent climbs require just as much preparation and planning as the first climb. Just as every campaign and event will require the same level of preparation and planning and time. The only difference between the first event and subsequent events is your experience, and that will impact your pace and your goals. Whether we are talking about climbing 9,000 feet in eight miles or raising $1 million dollars in twelve months, both are quite a feat.

Understanding Your Surroundings

To become an effective fundraiser, you need to understand the culture at the non-profit. Whether you move up through the program side and are put in a position of leadership or come from outside the organization, understanding the culture is extremely valuable.

Professional and Personal Development

Many development personnel are solo acts. As a result, you may not have someone who is guiding you and ensuring you are getting the knowledge you need for long-term success. Not just your individual long-term success, but also for the long-term success of your organization.

Make time every week to invest in you. Here are some ideas:

- Find a blog that provides nourishment for your professional development;
- Find a blog that promotes your personal development.
- Find a podcast that entertains and educates, one you can listen to while you are carrying out other duties. Personally, I listen to old-time radio dramas, such as "Johnny Dollar" and "Dragnet" because I find they also help me with my storytelling.
- Once a month, connect with a mentor and solicit his or her opinion on a challenging subject for one hour.
- Once a year, find a conference or educational opportunity and ask your organization to invest in you. Many colleges and universities sponsor sessions specific to fundraising. Also, trade organizations,

including the Association of Fundraising Professionals, have regular meetings and learning opportunities.

As much as these activities contribute to your personal and professional growth, they play a role in your mental health, as well. It is important that you feel challenged and growing in your role—that is the value of blogs and podcasts. You also need to share experiences, thus the value of regular meetings and conferences with other fundraisers. We all need to have an outlet to release stress and laugh, and that is why I recommend humorous podcasts. One of my favorite books, which takes a humorist's view of fundraising, is *May I Cultivate You* by Philip Perdue.

There are a couple of research pieces that share one day of training for a development professional usually yields between $25,000–$40,000 in additional results. Who can argue with this type of return on investment?

You'll read more about setting up a training plan in Chapter 2.

MacGyver is Not a Compliment

"MacGyver" was a TV show in the 1980s that has recently been revived; it's about a guy who could fix anything with a Swiss army knife, a paperclip, and duct tape, along with any other items that are within his reach. One thing that non-profit practitioners become adept at is doing with only what they have in front of them. Many are skilled at finding the latest free versions of software to help them with graphic design or event planning and marketing. Many hoard decorations and centerpieces from previous events to save on expenses.

Often, you fundraisers make it look so easy. No one will see the stress you go, through seeking donations of "stuff" because your budget is half of what you need. They will not understand why your kids think you are addicted to Pinterest because you are trying to find the least costly way to provide the WOW! factor at your next event. This is with no regard for the countless hours it will cost you to save a $100 to $200. It is unbelievable the number of $500 sponsorships that are traded for what costs a business only $50 or $100. That is nuts.

You are a real MacGyver when you are able to use your donor management system and come up with $10,000 or $50,000 or $100,000 in a pinch. It is easier to get motivated to save $100 on some centerpieces because that provides some instant gratification. However you were hired to raise money for your organization's mission, not to showcase your crafting ability. When you get ready to invest hours on crafts, take time to evaluate if instead, you could raise $1000 in the same time you could save $200. Which is a better use of your time?

It Will Be Emotional

You are working with an amazing organization that has an incredible mission. Your job is to tell stories that motivate people's hearts to give to your organization. These stories will impact you and will motivate you to do more.

In Chapter 7, I share the parable of the starfish. It's the story of a young boy who is focused on making a difference for just one starfish, not all the ones that wash up on shore. Making a difference for just one is all our donors are trying to accomplish. Whether that is one disaster victim being served, one rescued animal, one person receiving individual care, or one plot of land that is left a little greener. That statistic of "one" needs to be your resolve. Eventually, you will help several at one time, and based on your skill level, that may be more appropriate. However, with all that you will witness, all you can do is your job, which is to raise money.

The Truth

So here is the truth about the position you are in: Fundraising is a sales position!

Don't make that face.

You are selling the idea that you and the organization, in partnership with the donor, can make a difference. In reality, everyone is in sales. You have to sell yourself to your partner, your prospective employer, and a little bit to your friends and neighbors. To proclaim a belief or an idea as it relates to a product or an entity and receive funding as a result means that you are in sales.

Before those who have been in fundraising, development, advancement, and philanthropy (or one of the many other designations) may make a decision to stop reading this book, let me say that fundraising is also many other things.

In the Twenty-first Century, fundraising is so much more than its roots. Fundraising dates back to several origins: the compassion of religious communities to serve those in need; the American Red Cross assisting those impacted by war; or the wisdom of Andrew Carnegie and John Rockefeller to understand their obligation to "give back."

One of the earliest stories of fundraising is in the Twelfth Century. St. John of Matha raised funds from the noble community he was once a part of to purchase Christians, who had been captured and sold into slavery, so he could set them free.

Today, non-profit organizations are integral parts of our communities, doing important work that includes research, helping the poor, and inspiring entrepreneurs. In recent years, work in charitable organizations has become a career for professionals, not just a volunteer role for community members.

Fundraising is a career. Now, community colleges and universities have courses focused on non-profit management and fundraising. There are multiple professional organizations that promote the profession. The private business community (along with the non-profit community) is recognizing the parallels between charities and business. It is much more than a spin-off from religious organizations or bands of committed community members meeting around kitchen tables.

Fundraising is an opportunity. To those who want to create and support change, fundraising provides donors with the opportunities to do just that through their "time, talent, and treasure." Fundraising, in whatever form, provides the organized opportunity for individuals and organizations to make an impact with their collective support.

In their book, *Rainmaking*, Roy Jones and Andrew Olsen identify the job of fundraising as the "Philanthropic Matchmaker." They say, "[I] take compassionate, caring people and match them with worthy successful programs to create partnerships that help improve our communities." I call that creating the right opportunity . . . for the donor, the organization, and the community.

Fundraising is storytelling. It is the ability to share information and the impact of your organization through a great story. Great stories allow people to identify with your mission through the ways a client or community has been impacted, providing a portal where they can replace your protagonist with a family member, a neighbor, themselves, or their community. Like the parable of the starfish, impact stories provide the opportunity for donors to recognize that they can make a difference.

Fundraising is a strategy. When there are more than 1.5 million non-profits in the United States alone, survival means having a plan. A strategy. There are many worthy causes created by people with the best of intentions, but how will you ensure the resolve of your organization over that of other non-profits? Do you understand your costs? Do you know your impact? Can you share your story?

Fundraising is a process. In professional fundraising, there is a process called "moves management," which was established by the development office at Cornell University. It is the moving of a prospective donor from cultivation to solicitation and into stewardship. It is a "quality driven approach to relationship management" according to R. Daniel Shepherd that identifies the difference between activities that cultivate a donor and activities that move a donor through a process to make an impactful and significant gift.

These steps often parallel the steps involved in sales processes taught at major organizations or by significant sales trainers, such as Brian Tracy, Zig Ziglar, or Jeffrey Gitomer. Significant sales organizations, including Pfizer, ADP, and GM, invest in their sales teams with time, training, and commitment to these processes. Bloomerang, a donor management platform did a report several years ago that showed training for development professionals will increase their success by $37,000.

Fundraising is important. Through fundraising, we empower individuals and organizations to work together to make a difference. Sometimes, that difference is in the hometown; sometimes, that difference is a world away. However, through combined efforts we help supporters virtually travel and make an impact.

Without our organizations and the vehicles we provide, life-saving research could not be discovered. Communities that have been devastated would struggle to be rebuilt. Some leaders would not have received the education that developed them. The poor would remain hungry and homeless.

I believe . . . Fundraising is sales with a purpose. Many in our profession want to suggest this is just not true. Some will argue that it is similar but not the same. One person suggested that fundraising was more about customer service. Customer service is just a form of inside sales. Every successful organization has a successful sales front line.

"Sales" and "to sell," are not a dirty words. It is a noble profession (one held by many of your donors). For many, it is a career. I have often commented that fundraisers make the best sales people because they possess an inherent characteristic of the best sales people. They *believe* in their product. Many have a personal connection with their organization and feel rewarded by the people they serve beyond what any commission check could provide.

When you think about the revenue individual sales people are asked to generate in one year and the amount an individual fundraiser is asked to raise, they are very comparable. In some occasions, what an individual fundraiser is responsible for is equivalent to that of an entire sales team.

Fundraising is done without a product (like a widget) but with the affinity of donors. Many fundraisers do it on their own, without a marketing department or constituent support team. They are it. They are superstars.

For charitable and non-profit organizations, the fundraising team is the frontline sales team. Sales and their processes are unique in every industry, but there are fundamentals that apply. Just as pharmaceutical sales is specific and defined by its role in the healthcare industry, so fundraising is specific and defined by the not-for-profit industry.

Each industry's sales teams are the front line in building awareness and demonstrating the need for their goods and services. As fundraisers, we are constantly working to engage people to share the amazing stories of our cause. We are the people on the front line, building value and awareness for our organization.

Preparing to Climb versus Reaching the Top

Preparing to climb and climbing the mountain is the bulk of attacking a mountain. Mounting the summit or reaching the top is the shortest part of that whole process. The same is true in fundraising. There are many tasks—much planning and preparation—that go into fundraising, and then there is the "asking for money" part.

I do not recommend asking for money without the planning, preparation, and practice that go into fundraising. Just as Ed Barnard encourages those interested in reaching the top of Rainier to take the necessary steps to prepare for their climbs, *Fundraising Is: Everything Done Before Asking for Money* is meant to be a reference book. One should be able to go to any chapter and find the material needed for the subject referenced.

The toolbox at the end of each chapter will help you quickly identify the key ideas discussed in each chapter. It is also how one can put the concepts of the chapter into action.

The definitions in the back of the book are tools to train other members of your organization. Using these definitions will help everyone have a shared understanding.

CHAPTER 2

COMING INTO THE LIGHT

In the movie *Renaissance Man*, Bill Rago (Danny DeVito's character) is an award-winning ad-man who was laid off. The employment office finds him a short-term gig as an instructor at a military base. When he arrives on base, he has to park at the entrance and hoof it to his building in the interior of the campus. Getting disoriented, he asks a soldier for directions. The soldier provides directions in soldier speak, classifying distances in "clicks" and using acronyms for the landmarks.

Bill Rago sarcastically responds to the soldier's question, "Got it?" by asking the soldier, "Can I buy a vowel?" In frustration, Rago throws his hands up, and points the question, "This way?" and the soldier begins to repeat his directions the same way.

No matter our level of training, years of experience, or knowledge of the position we are walking into, there is a learning curve. For some, that curve is short, and for others it's long. There are many things that contribute to its length. Part of the curve is in our control, but we often inherit many influencers outside our control. Some of these factors include the organization of information at the non-profit, the communication that occurs from the people we work with, and whether there is currently any organized training at the non-profit.

When I went to work for Enterprise Rent-A-Car, the new employees spent two days in the classroom learning how to use the computer system, represent the products, and understand the glossary of terms (explanation of inside lingo). Do you have any idea what a LOFR is? That is rental car speak for lube oil filter and tire rotation. When I left Enterprise twelve years later, new hires received an even greater foundation by spending an entire week in the classroom.

In every position I have had, there is a series of systems and terminology that any new team member needed to learn. In addition, I had to understand what the workflows, processes, and protocols were. I needed to comprehend what the focus and primary strategies were, what was measured, and more specifically, what I would be measured on. Like Bill Rago in *Renaissance Man,* who needed to learn about working on a military base in addition to making a career change, many of us need to understand our new environment as much as we need to understand our role in that environment.

Then, of course, there is the office culture, or the office politics, per se. What are the rules and how do things really get accomplished? I feel like I have always exceled in this aspect of any position. This is because of the value I have always placed on people and relationships. I talk more about the value of relationships, both intra- and inter- organization, in Chapter 8.

As I stated in the previous chapter, the amount of revenue you, as a fundraiser, are expected to generate is comparable to the performance goals of a highly compensated salesperson. You have belief and passion as your cause. You are also motivated. That, in part, is why you are reading this book.

Getting Organized

There is a great scene at the start of the movie *Hoosiers.* Coach Dale comes in to his first practice, and the volunteer coach tries to tell him how things are run. Coach Dale stops practice and tells the players it is not about how well they shoot; it is about the fundamentals, and he has two weeks until the first game. Coach Dale is confident in what he is doing and gets plenty of pushback, but this team has never made it past a round or two of sectional competition. For those two weeks, coach drills on passing, teamwork, and endurance and focuses on getting to know and understand his team.

Understanding that fundraising is 85 percent everything you do *before* you ask for money is similar to Coach Dale demonstrating that building stamina and ball control is more important than shooting (you still have to shoot the ball to score points). In fundraising, understanding the mission and defining the impact is more important than asking for money (but you still need to ask for money—in most cases—to raise it).

If no one has provided you with a training plan or a training calendar, the following is a suggested calendar to use. If you have been in your position for a while, look at the following as a checklist you can use to ensure you have received the guidance required to build a solid foundation for your position. If you are looking at hiring a new employee, think about creating your own calendar to establish a solid foundation for your co-worker, team member, protégé, or successor.

This calendar at the conclusion of this chapter is a refined version of the activities I did when I joined the Red Cross. It is also the one I put together for new fundraisers I have been involved in hiring. This calendar is designed to build a solid foundation to make people stronger fundraisers for the organization. I've outlined how I would execute this calendar, but any way you use this calendar will set you up for success.

Just like most corporations, which invest approximately eleven days in the first six months of a professional salesperson, this training plan does the same, spreading the time over half days during the first several weeks.

Discover and own the plan. Whether you are the first person in a position or replacing a person, most likely the organization has been doing some form of fundraising before you got there. There is a record of how they have raised funds. If the plan is recorded, review it and understand your role. If it is not recorded, start documenting the plan. It is important to be aware of what has been raised each month for the previous twelve months, when events have occurred and their details (attendance, expenses, results), and when solicitations have been sent out. These are just a few of the basic questions you should have about a plan.

Learning this information and laying this groundwork will require some research. If there has been an event in the past, there is bound to be some indicators. There may be a file that has information in it. A poster or program flyer could be stuck amongst other files. When you look at what was raised in a month, there may be an abnormally large group of donor or entries on a date that may be an indicator of an event or solicitation. When you interview staff and volunteers, asking about these dates may be a vital part of your interview.

Know the mission. Spend at least four hours a week for the first few months directly learning and personally experiencing your mission. When I started with the Red Cross, this was one of the best things I did. I met with the disaster team; I observed CPR classes; I went to military services events; and I spent a day at a blood drive. It would be great if you could do it all in a week, but it is never that convenient. If you ask around, you can begin to place these activities on your schedule before you get too busy with your role in the organization. Through these activities, you will gain your own stories to share with donors.

Build a glossary of terms. Every time you raise your eyebrows at a term, or need to clarify and ask what an acronym means, stop and make a note of it. If you need it explained, so will donors, future volunteers, funders, other stakeholders, and future staff members. Those who come after you will appreciate it.

Every time I start a new job, every time I begin working with a new organization, I am always amazed at the volume of information there is to learn about the product or the mission. There are more than 200 safety features on cars, many that we are not aware of. There are too many pieces of personal protective equipment (PPE), and many of them are things we use everyday. Just like in product sales, there is an overload of information and lingo, such as PPE. When talking about your mission, there is lingo and overwhelming amounts of information. Regardless if you're discussing disaster management, addiction and recovery, domestic abuse, mental health, or education, there is more subject-specific language than you can imagine when it comes to delivering your mission. Add that to all the lingo and terminology for non-profits alone, such as the federal and state regulations and programs. In Virginia, every charity that wants to solicit funds needs to register with VDACS (Virginia Department of Agriculture and Consumer Services), for example.

Interview colleagues (volunteers and staff). Take the time to understand what other people in your organization do and how they came to join the organization. Again, you will begin to gather stories you can share with donors. Ask about challenges they face or task or ideas they would appreciate from the development team. You probably will not have any solutions, or maybe you can immediately respond, but you could just be the first person to ask. Be sure to listen and follow up if they comment.

Remember, most people are interested in assisting or helping. Not many enjoy the concept of being interviewed or responding to what you need. With that in mind, open your conversation with, "I wonder if you could help me?" This usually gets a better response than "I want to interview you" or "I need to interview you" or "I need this information from you."

Interview long-term significant donors. These donors may "belong" to other members of the development team, but ask them to take you on a visit. Talk to them like investors, the people responsible for funding your mission. Inquire about what they like about the organization and what they see as missed opportunities. Understand why they support the organization. Then for your benefit, ask them who else you should talk to or who do they think is a good prospect for the organization to invite to be a donor.

Be present. It will take time for you to get up and running for your organization. Along with reviewing records and identifying donors to talk to, make time to be a part of things going on in the office. This could be stuffing envelopes or verifying a deposit or editing a letter or even emptying the trash. Demonstrate that you want to be part of the team.

Most importantly, set goals. At the end of the first six weeks, you should have some idea of what you want to accomplish. Hopefully, you have been given a personal goal, and you have discovered ways you can accomplish those goals. If you have not been given a personal goal, then take time to develop two or three. Determine and write down how you plan to accomplish them and share these goals with some of the people you interviewed. This process will make your goals real and create accountability.

The Toolbox

When my son was eight, my parents gave him a toolbox for Christmas. He always enjoyed being a part of my DIY projects and built amazing things with Legos. The gift seemed appropriate. They went to Lowes and asked the salesperson in the red and blue vest for recommendations for toolboxes and what to put in it. He started with a kid's toolkit, but my father explained that this was going to be part of his gifts for years to come.

Thinking it was a great idea (good enough for him to do for his own grandkids), The Lowes's rep recommended a lightweight hammer and a pair of pliers to start. My mom, thinking it would still be pretty empty, wanted to get him a set of screw drivers, The Lowes guy suggested a magnetic level, sharing there was less chance of loosing an eye.

I like this story because it is a good analogy for many of my clients. When I get the privilege to work with them, I often walk in with an empty toolbox, one ready to be filled with just the right tools for them to become productive in fundraising, especially in Major Gifts.

You do not need to fill your toolbox immediately, nor do you need to be proficient with a tool right away. At the conclusion of each chapter, you will find a brief section that will focus on key take-a-ways for that chapter. These are compiled into a bonus section that also includes helpful links to some additional resources.

Start filling your toolbox.

A sample NEW HIRE training plan

Use this checklist for any development new hire, regardless of his or her stage in this career. A new-hire training plan is focused on getting people familiar with your organization through a coordinated plan, one focused on setting them up for long-term success. After the first week, roughly eight hours each week should be committed to your professional development as a part of the organization.

Week 1

	Task	Activity/ Plan
☐	Gov't paperwork	
☐	Organization paperwor	• Conflict of interests • Confidentiality agreement
☐	Facility/ Office Tour	
☐	Meet key staff	
☐	Review Mission statement History of the organization Bi-laws	
☐	Discuss job description	Review specific tasks Review expected schedule
☐	Identify development plan	
☐	Research history of activities	

- [ ] Receive access to necessary systems and facilities
- [ ] Begin learning Donor Management System
- [ ] Begin learning internal systems and protocols for programs/ client impact
- [ ] Begin setting appointments with Volunteer Leadership

Week 2

	Task	Activity/ Plan
[ ]	Set at least 2 appointments with volunteer leadership	
[ ]	Begin pulling reports from Donor Management System	Any reports like top donors.
[ ]	Identify opportunities to observe mission related that you are raising money for.	Spend at least 2 hours observing. Collect your own stories to share with donors

	Task	Activity/ Plan
☐	Spend 1 hour with online education	Participate in a webinar for your Donor Management, read a few blogs

Week 3

	Task	Activity/ Plan
☐	Role-play interactions with volunteer leadership and top donors	Interact with someone that can provide intelligence on volunteers and donors and interested in your success (Like the person who hired you)
☐	Set at least 2 appointments with volunteer leadership	
☐	Pull report on top donors and discuss with staff	
☐	Make at least 2 appointments with top and/or long-term donors	

	Task	Activity/ Plan
☐	Identify opportunities to observe programs that you are raising money for.	Spend at least 2 hours observing. Collect your own stories to speak with donors
☐	Spend 1 hour with online education	Participate in a webinar for your Donor Management, read a few blogs

Week 4

	Task	Activity/ Plan
☐	Continue role-playing (practice) interactions with top donors and volunteers	
☐	Set at least 2 appointments with volunteer leadership	
☐	Make at least 2 appointments with top and/or long-term donors	

☐ Pull reports on monthly contributions for the previous 12 months	
☐ Identify opportunities to observe programs that you are raising money for.	Spend at least 2 hours observing. Collect your own stories to speak with donors
☐ Spend 1 hour with online education	Participate in a webinar for your Donor Management, read a few blogs

Week 5

Task	Activity/ Plan
☐ From your monthly reports set goals for your first year	Use Specific Measurable Attainable Relevant Time-bound
☐ Continue Role-play (practice) interactions with top donors and volunteers	
☐ Set at least 2 appointments with volunteer leadership	
☐ Make at least 2 appointments with top and/or long-term donors	

☐	Set appointment with other departments and ask for candor and feedback	Find the bright spots and opportunities to work positively together.
☐	Identify opportunities to observe programs that you are raising money for.	
☐	Spend 1 hour with online education	

Week 6

	Task	Activity/ Plan
☐	Set additional goals beyond funds raised (2 or 3) for growth and development. For example: meet with 10 donors weekly.	No more than 5 total goals
☐	Include action steps	Action steps are how you plan to achieve the goals you have set forth

☐	Sign-up for a Class or professional organization meeting like the Assoc. of Fundraising Professionals.	You can find local AFP chapters at https://afpglobal.org/chapters. The value of these classes is in as much of the people you will have to meet as much of the information they provide.
☐	Continue to set appointments for the future with donors and leadership. Attempt to have 5 or more face to face activities each week	
☐	Share your goals	Create accountability for yourself by sharing your goals with colleagues and ask for their help in achieving them.

⚒ TOOLBOX ⚒

Development Plan—Understand how your organization plans to raise the needed funds for its mission on paper. You can do it as you go, but it is best if you layout and continually record results over the next twelve months. More on this in Chapter 4.

Training plan—If you are just starting out in fundraising or have arrived at a new organization, before you do anything else, put a plan in place for the next sixty days and make a commitment. If you have been in your current position for awhile and feel your foundation was lacking, create a plan for the next one hundred days, and make the same commitment following the guidelines in this chapter.

- Learn the organization mission—understand its impact, who the organization serves, and how it is accomplished
- Build a glossary of terms—any time you need someone to explain a term or an acronym, put it on paper because someone else will need it explained. We have started a glossary in the appendix of this book.
- Interviews—sit down with fellow staff, longtime volunteers, and significant donors. This will help you understand the culture of the organization.
- Cross-train—learn and participate in other departments . . . everything from emptying the trash to setting up and attending volunteer training. It will aid in talking with prospects and donors.
- Have goals—you need your own goals that will help the organization achieve its goals. This will help you appreciate the value of your role to the organization.

Chapter 3

Answering the Call

Do you remember the first time someone asked you what you wanted to be when you grew up? Was a professional fundraiser even on your radar?

Whatever your response was, I am sure it had something to do with making a difference or helping people. It might be safe to assume that some personal life experience impacted you to put you in this position of helping others. It could have been a disease that impacted you or a loved one or a tragedy you believe was preventable—"if only!" For example, you had to watch a family member deteriorate physically while receiving chemotherapy and fighting cancer and manage the emotion you felt each time you saw them. Whether it was the loss of hair or weight as they endured the chemo or the return to their "old self" after the chemo, it impacted you, Perhaps it was a family member dealing with addiction and the many things that may go along with that, such as the lies, theft, absence of that loved one, or the concern associated with criminal activity. A million reasons could have brought you to this doorway. Take a moment to identify them, name them, and own them.

For me, it was in Boy Scouts. With a little coaching from my mother, I would get dressed in my scout uniform and go around the neighborhood, selling fertilizer to raise funds for my troop. It was easy; people were going to buy fertilizer anyway, so they figured they might as well get a tax-deductible donation for it (not that I really understood what deductions meant at age thirteen). When I had conquered the neighborhood and ended up selling more than the next two people combined, I wanted to sell even more. So I contacted family and some of my parents' friends. My first year, I sold around 150 bags of fertilizer, paid for my summer camp, and was the hero of the troop. By the time I had stopped selling fertilizer, I had sold around 500 bags and may still hold the record. I thought this meant I was good at sales, so I started reading sales legends, including Zig Ziglar and Jeffrey Gitomer. I read about all sorts of successful salespeople and interviewed a family friend who owned a car dealership. I was committed to my success as a salesperson. Every time there was a fundraiser for school, I was at or near the top (except for cash raffles, YUCK!).

It took me years to understand what exactly about the successful sales experience was so motivating; it was the impact that drove me. Understanding how I helped to make a difference made me a better salesperson. In my professional career, my numbers were always higher when I was able to make "a greater" impact with my results. The impact was more than the personal benefit of buying the latest device or taking a fun trip. It was the one that benefited others, not just myself. Making a real change for my customers really drove me.

One of my most common statements is, "Fundraising is sales with a purpose." When the Red Cross gave me the opportunity to serve, and I was able to use my sales techniques and exceed goals, I felt as if I had answered a call. About ten years prior to me landing at the Red Cross, I had sat in a neighbor's living room as he asked me, "Have you ever thought about a career in fundraising?"

Since that time in the Scouts, I made a commitment to personal development and took advantage of every opportunity. I attended seminars, signed up for training, became a sales trainer, and constantly worked on my craft. That was in sales, but was it only sales? The syntax changes slightly, but both sales and fundraising function in similar ways. They are both about creating revenue. One uses the term persuasion, the other motivation. Success in both is highly dependent on one's ability to cultivate relationships.

Fortunately, I started in fundraising when webinars, blogs, and resources were abundantly available online. The world of fundraising was becoming focused as a profession and working to establish itself as a career path. Even though groups, such as the Association of Fundraising Professionals, have been around for decades, the profession itself is still growing.

One of the many challenges for professionals in fundraising is the small shop. It's the situation where a non-profit may have a dozen or so people on staff but only a handful of full time fundraisers—maybe only one tasked with the responsibility of raising a bulk of the revenue needs. Unlike major corporations, such as Enterprise, which have teams of support people and salespeople, who have the redundancy and resources to offer training. The mindset of a major corporation is if you want to make more money, you need more and better-trained salespeople. The frontline is an investment. In charitable organizations, fundraisers are considered overhead, and you can't risk higher overhead to raise more money (even just for the short-term).

As a solo fundraiser or member of a small team, not only do you have to be aware of the next major donor, you have to be aware of personal and professional development opportunities, especially low-cost or free ones. These opportunities help a fundraiser remain innovative, build resources, and raise more money.

Your education in this profession is very important and has significant impact. In 2016, Bloomerang and DonorSearch funded a research project authored by Dr. Adrian Seargent, Amy Eisenstein, ACFRE, and Dr. Rita Koscaz called "Major Gift Fundraising: Unlocking the Potential for Smaller Non-profits." In this report, they concluded that regular professional development correlated to an average $37,000 increase in revenue per fundraiser.

$37,000. I'm going to let that hang there for a moment.

Fundraising is sales. Sometimes, it is not all about selling the mission to your donors but about selling a concept to your leadership (paid and volunteer). To help with your sales pitch to leadership, here are some reasons to promote professional development opportunities for yourself and your team.

Reduces turnover. Leadership needs to understand that providing the opportunity for professional development sends the message that they value staff and want to invest in their people. It is another form of compensation that yields results in multiple ways. In the *Clear Company* blog, they reference many statistics about the costs of turnover. One statistic they share is that even a minimum wage employee costs about $5500 + benefits. When discussing fundraising personnel, you add in the costs associated with the relationships they have formed and their ability to grow contributions or know about planned contributions they were working on, and this number skyrockets.

Provides results. Regardless of the number of conferences I attend, I always find a few golden nuggets. Sometimes, a nugget is a new software or report I find valuable. Other times, it is a bit of creativity that allows an organization to connect their mission with the donors or prospective donors. One time, it was a simple "trick" that resulted in over $800 in six months (twice the cost of the conference). The trick, suggested by a presenter, is to include a request for support in every staff members' email signature. I'm talking about a simple, "Please support our mission . . ." with a link to a donation page. All the contributions were from new donors. When the new donors were reviewed, it was discovered many of them had relationships with non-development staff.

More efficient. Whether it is as a result of relationships formed or knowledge gained, I have witnessed processes become more effective and greater results from people attending a class or a conference. Even if others don't necessarily see a difference or an immediate financial impact on results, it most often returns time to your staff member and improves morale. Knowledge gained often reduces costs and improves the bottom line in uncommon ways.

Remain Aware

As a fundraiser working at a small to midsize non-profit, your team may consist only of you and an executive director. In some circumstances, you may be so lucky as to have an administrative person or an events person. Whether it's just you or multiple people involved in fundraising, everyone has a responsibility to engage in professional development.

There are opportunities everywhere to improve your craft and grow in your knowledge and perspective as a professional. What follows are some suggestions for how you grow in this profession. Some professional development opportunities are very inexpensive, while others require some investment. Regardless of the expense, it will all be returned to you as a professional and to your organization. There is very little downside to personal growth. The only challenge will be to make the time for it.

Involve someone else. If you are in a small shop where you are the only fundraiser or there is just be one other person, be sure to include someone in your training process. This other person could be a peer at another organization or a mentor. Please recognize that a mentor is not always someone with more wisdom or experience. A mentor can be someone whose energy you find contagious and who challenges and encourages you.

Read. Congratulations! You are clearly committed to your professional development. Matthew Kelly, renowned business author and founder of Floyd Consulting, says that reading a book is one of the most cost-effective personal and professional development activities you can accomplish. If you read just five pages a day, you can read four to six books a year.

You can also read blogs, magazine articles, white papers, or numerous other mediums. Just do it every day.

Use existing resources. If you have a cloud-based donor management system, chances are high they have a blog with helpful resources. They may also offer webinars that provide more information than just how to use their software. If you joined a local association, they usually have roundtables, which are as valuable as what you bring to the session. Be sure to participate. Some of the most valuable information you can receive is from fellow non-profit executives.

Join a group. It could be a networking group, civic group, chamber, or professional association. These associations and groups often sponsor worthwhile sessions that help you connect with other non-profits and business leaders in the area. They also sponsor research and webinars, which are limited to members only. Membership often pays for itself in the relationships and the knowledge shared through those relationships.

Take a class/attend a conference. Formal instruction offers access to material that can be referred to regularly. It also has value in the connections you can make with other people in the class or at the conference. The value of these educational opportunities is often amplified if you invest a little bit of "yourself" in these activities.

Take a class/attend a conference outside of fundraising. There are many great organizations that train people and offer ideas and principles, which can be applied to fundraising. One that comes to mind is the Disney Leadership Institute, a great education on outstanding service and connecting individually with your guest (like you would want to connect with donors). Another is a Zig Ziglar seminar that focuses on relationship selling, which can educate you on how to leverage relationships to yield greater results.

Hire a consultant. This may seem like a shameless plug, but an outside perspective can be very useful. Consultants carry the wisdom of many organizations and often have observed the challenges you face at other organizations where they have worked. Consultants don't only provide results in increased funds raised, but also in time saved and reduced costs.

In addition to all these, there are accreditation opportunities, such as earning your Certified Fund Raising Executive (CFRE) or participating in continuing education programs through local colleges and universities. Resources are available at FundraisingIs.net/bookresources. Always be open to any opportunity to learn.

⚒ TOOLBOX ⚒

Own Your Development—You are your own key to success. Take time to look for opportunities to grow as a person and a professional. Here are some ideas:

- Read daily
- Join a group or professional association
- Take a class within and outside your profession
- Hire a consultant/ coach.

Engage a peer—Whether you engage them as a mentor or just a sounding board, make a commitment to sit down with them for ninety minutes, once a month. If all you have is those ninety minutes, then set an agenda. This will help you feel focused and accomplished during your time together. It is also OK not to cover everything on your agenda. We are all a little ambitious in what we want to accomplish. Plus it may encourage you to connect more often.

Grow within your organization annually, at least one time a year:

- Learn about your organization
- Learn about the budget process
- Spend a day in one of your programs
- Attend a board or advisory committee meeting
- Do something so that you gain knowledge and better understand those you raise money for.

A detailed list of resources and professional development ideas are included at **Fundraising.net/bookresources**.

CHAPTER 4

THE PLAN

I enjoy the movies. I also enjoy great stories. As we talk about planning, a great planner (schemer) comes to mind: Kevin McAllister. Yes, the screaming kid from the *Home Alone* movie. Toward the end of the movie, Kevin runs in the front door, locks it, looks into the camera, and declares, "This is my house. I must defend it!" In the next scene, he clears a desk and rolls out his "BATTLE PLAN" to defend the house. It is detailed, color-coded, and specific.

I love this as an inspiration for creating a development plan because it is detailed, easy to read, and specific. I am sure there are other movies I could use as an example that involve intricate plan, including Ocean's movies, the *Great Escape*, *The Dirty Dozen*, *Catch That Kid* or a dozen others. However, *Home Alone* is the only movie I can remember that has such a visual and memorable "plan" that we see on paper, which is then executed.

In Chapter 2, one of the first things I suggest for your self-imposed training plan is to know and own the development plan. There may be one that has existed on paper, and if it does then bring it out and review it. If it is not on paper, then find a way to record it and make it detailed, easy to read and specific.

Developing Your Plan

A solid plan and a clear goal are the footing and foundation of the shop you build as the professional fundraiser in your organization. As you review and build your plan, the following are some key ingredients to remember.

The goal. Is there a clear goal for your development plan? In addition to the annual revenue goal, are there monthly revenue goals and event goals for revenue? Do all these smaller goals equal your annual goal? Do they exceed the annual goal? How about the non-revenue activities, such as the "feel good" events or social media? Do they have relevant goals, including number of attendees or engagements, which support your revenue aspirations?

Who is involved? Have you shared your plan with others? Have you involved others in your planning? Is your plan a living and breathing document that is aligned or involved with other departments' plans?

What is its relationship? Does this plan roll up into the organization's strategic plan? What other departments does your plan directly support? How have the goals been established? Was it just an increase over the previous year, or is it based on the identified needs of the organization? For instance, does it align with an increase in the number of people served or perhaps the establishment of a new program? When your plan has a relationship to these tangible activities, then it motivates all involved because it is about more than just the dollars; it is about the stories and the people.

It Requires Some Assembly

A very vivid story comes to mind as I think about putting together a solid plan. I was excited to get my first real piece of adult furniture, an entertainment center. It was the 90s, and I had invested in a 27" TV to go along with my component stereo system. This was to replace the cinder blocks and 2x4s to properly display my impressive electronics. I was so proud.

It arrived! I had forgotten about the "some assembly required." It was in a tall, thin box, and it was HEAVY! So heavy I needed to wait for my roommate to get home to get it to our third-floor apartment (in a building with no elevator). Luckily, neither of us developed a hernia.

Then I had to assemble this piece of furniture. I measured to make sure it was not going to take up more floor space than the blocks and wood it was replacing. I did not count on the space required to assemble it. It would take over the living room, and I would spend an entire day putting it together.

In my head, I had seen the perfection of my first piece of real furniture. I had missed so many steps in achieving that perfection. If I had slowed down and paid attention to information, such as the shipping weight or the suggested assembly time, I would have carved out three times the proposed assembly time and not had any other plans.

I was so focused on the end result; I did not evaluate all the costs or requirements necessary to accomplish my desired end. Requirements, such as the amount of time it required to assemble it, the strain it placed on my relationship with my roommate as our small apartment was overtaken by this assembly, or the shear frustration of moving this monstrosity out of the apartment when we moved out and into three other homes. If I would have only paid attention to some details and planned better.

Planning Today Saves Time Tomorrow

Planning is valuable and can often save a lot of wasted energy and time. Today, companies invest a great deal of money in planning sessions and retreats. Organizations hire consultants to come in and help them develop annual plans for fundraising.

Often, I meet with organizations, and they have created very detailed plans. However, they soon collect dust and aren't reviewed after the day they were printed. Hopefully, the instructions in this chapter will create a plan that becomes as much a part of your team as the overenthusiastic volunteer who seems irreplaceable but also drives you nuts.

I believe great plans include goals, measurements, and foresight. Like the metaphor of a map, you have to know where you are heading and that means establishing a clear goal. Like the assembly of the entertainment center, if I had reviewed more of the information, I could have planned for people to help me assemble it or more people to help move it up to the apartment. You plan to have some result at the end. With building plans, you plan to have a structure that meets your needs. With a personal trainer, you have a plan to lose weight and improve your health. Your development plan is to meet the revenue and awareness needs of your mission.

Start with the goals. You need to know what you are working toward. I have always found the acronym SMART (Specific Measurable Attainable Relevant and Time-Bound) to be extremely useful. SMART goals are not a new concept. Your goal should always be a stretch. If you achieve your goal, it is truly a celebration, but be able to celebrate if you get a B+ or an A- (85–90 percent of your goal). At that percentage, you still meet or slightly exceed the needs of your mission.

Small and incremental goals are as important as your overall goal. Achieving smaller goals often provides the motivation for larger goals and makes the overall goal seem within reach. These are often activities, including donor meetings or social media posts, that are necessary to meet your larger revenue goal. These could be goals for attendance at Friendraising events, events that are focused on awareness more than revenue. Even the number of responses from a solicitation can be as valuable as the dollars raised. Anything you can track will help you measure success.

Setup your calendar. Fundraising is everything you do to gather support and tell the story of your organization to build value. 85 percent of all fundraising is done before the first penny is asked for, thus the title of this book.

Using a calendar format (see below), include everything you will do this year that involves asking for money, engaging your donors, or sharing your story.

ABC Community Organization
Development Calendar   Goal: $420,000

Month	Engagement	Ask	Communication	Soc. Media	Planning
July 2018 *$35,000* 2019 *$53,049*	9 - New Employee Training 12 - Parent Orientation	9 - Staff giving Goal: *$32,500* Act: *$30,120*	12 - Handout (Giving Catalog) 20 - Email Newsletter	- Golf Tourney - Orientation - Classroom Prep - New Families - School Mission	10 - Final contributions to email N/L 31 - Finalize Volunteers for Golf
August 2018 *$30,082* 2019 *$34,364*	25 - Prayer at the Pole 29 - Golf Tourney	29 - Golf Goal: *$10,000* Act: *$16,067*		- Golf Tourney - Thank Golf Sponsors - Welcom Back - New Staff	- Recruit Table Capt for Spring Breakfast - Identify impact stories for year-end report
Sept 2018 *$50,017* 2019 *$39,738*	18- Grandparent Day 21 - Board Thank-a-thon 27 - TC training	18 - GP Day Goal: *$12,000* Act: *$8340*	10 - Golf thank you packets 21 - Board Thank-a-thon	- Thank Golf Attendees - GP day - Thankathon - TC Training - Student retreat	10 - Sched appt with Church Partners 25 - Finalize Founder's day

List all your direct engagement opportunities you can have with a donor or a prospective donor. Anything that would be a program highlight (graduations, performances) would be a donor highlight. These often are not donor-focused events but mission-focused activity where donors have the chance to observe the outcomes of their support.

Include any way you are going to communicate with your supporters, such as direct mail, email, or posters. This could include paid advertising.

Some people have a separate social media column to make sure they remember to post about important activities and share the story. Social media also gives you immediate information about community response to your posts. It is a great source for learning what messages resonate with supporters.

Non-profits have a significant dependency on public contributions. It is important that you know when and how you are soliciting contributions. You should also know what the goals are for each "hard" solicitation.

- Hard—A direct asks for support through an event or activity.
- Soft—An opportunity to support the organization as the part of another activity like a donate button as part of a newsletter

Events are often hard asks. For your event to achieve their goals, they often require a great deal of effort and planning. That is where the planning column on an overall calendar is valuable. By including deadlines and other information in a single location, it allows you to be proactive rather than reactive.

The value of events is how you engage participants following the event. A goal should be to get 5 percent to 10 percent of the participants to engage and donate to the organization after the event. It is valuable to gather information on every participant who attends your events. Plan post-event communication.

Whether we are discussing "asks", events, donor engagement, or even the decision to hold or not hold an event for the organization, there are a multitude of tasks and activities that need to occur in the many months prior to any event/campaign. This calendar is not just for you and your team but should be a communication tool for board and leadership, as well.

Make sure no details are missed and others are informed by including deadlines and decision dates (invitations going out, confirming catering, sending programs to print) in the PLANNING column. This allows all of your activities to occur in the most professional way and with the least number of surprises. This makes a PLANNING column invaluable.

A sample calendar format is available at fundraisingis. net/bookresources.

Track Everything

There are many things that impact the success of your fundraising efforts. The more you track, the more you can understand how your efforts are impacted by your activities. Things to track:

- Funds raised as a result of activity (events, solicitation)
- Funds raised monthly
- Attendance at activities
- Engagements on social media
- Solicitation response

In his book, *Upstream: The Quest to Solve Problems Before They Happen*, Dan Heath breaks data into two categories: 1) Data for the purpose of learning and 2) Data for the purpose of inspection. Data for inspection is the most common and what we use for graphs and charts. It's often used to track progress at a glance. Data for the purpose of learning is the data most valuable to the people on the front lines. This is data that correlates with other things and helps to explain the impact. This data may be specific to the impact of client services or relationship building. For example, did donors, whom we visited, log an increase in contributions year over year versus donors we only communicated with digitally.

It takes both inspection and learning data to grow your development program.

Build Accountability

The cliché, "It takes a village," is true for any level of success. Individually, one can only achieve limited results. The more you engage others, the greater your results will be, and the greater you will want them to be. This is especially true when others are aware of your results and are cheering for your success.

For your own accountability, this plan cannot be a secret. It should be a reference point of every report. Instead of retyping what you have done or planning to do, you should update your development plan and just provide the plan. If needed, provide a short narrative that references the more complete development plan.

For other's accountability, this plan cannot be a secret. If you think you can solely raise a couple hundred thousand dollars or $1,000,000, then here is your wakeup call. For you to successfully accomplish any fundraising goal, it will take other people. Maybe it will take volunteers, administrative support, or program resources (like gathering those moving client stories) to achieve this goal. When you release and update the plan, you need to keep these support groups informed on what you need from them to accomplish the organization's goal.

If you can, keep your plan in a central location, such as a shared drive or a big whiteboard in your area, which everyone can see.

More than Money

As we review our annual plans, we can internalize the relationship so it is more than just a listing of numbers, dollars, and activities. Just as we try to educate donors on the impact of dollars, we need to do the same when discussing the impact of raising more money with our staff and involve them as part of the outcomes.

Do not just throw numbers out to be an increase over last year. Tie the amount you want to raise to a need. Possibilities for need could be a new program, a new staff position, or an increased number of clients who will benefit. It is even OK if you tie it to a raise for your staff, especially if there really has not been a significant raise for a while.

One of the groups I worked with helped me to see the value of setting benchmarks. As they achieved benchmarks in funding, they did little things like replacing the forty-year-old lobby and office furniture one piece at a time. You never knew how motivating new ergonomic office chairs could be. This got the staff excited about the development plan and helped build a "culture of philanthropy."

So as you look at that development plan from last year, start a conversation with the team. The team could be comprised of leadership or volunteers but must be people who will be involved in your plan. Ask, "If we got $50,000 more this year, how would you spend it?" Chances are, you will hear something that will make a difference for your organization.

Include individuals from outside the leadership or development team when you ask about an extra $50,000, $100,000, or more. Then when you talk about implementing a team member's (especially the idea of a non-fundraising team member) idea, you begin to build some of the relationships we will discuss in Chapter 9.

Many Plans Working Together

Just like the idea of being able to implement this plan on your own is a misnomer, so is the idea that this plan will function independently. This plan should roll up into the organization plan. If your organization does not have a long-term strategic plan, that is another book and at FundraisingIs.net/bookresources there are some of my favorite book recommendations on strategy.

Stewardship Plan—This is the activity/engagement you use to retain your donors. This needs to be detailed and segmented. It should also involve multiple levels of your organization, for instance:

- Executive Director contacts donors of gifts over $500
- Board member contact for gifts over $1000 and all long-term pledges
- Handwritten notes for all gifts over $200

When setting up this plan, here are some questions to consider: How will you acknowledge them? How will you show your impact? How will you engage your mid-level and upper-level donors versus your entry donors?

Cultivation Plan—This is about inviting people to learn more about your organization, especially individuals who attend your public events/fundraisers. Examples of ways you can engage people could be:

- Scheduling a regular tour and the entire staff may invite people, too
- Having regular "mission moments" that are posted to social media and demonstrate organization impact
- Creating a formal volunteer orientation that discusses all aspects of the organization, including fundraising

Cultivation can include your activity online (email and social media). It may also include a regular, outward-focused event that staff and leadership can invite colleagues or the public to attend.

A standard debrief. You need a way to evaluate your event/campaign. Involve your stakeholders in the evaluation. It should happen within five days following your event and should be placed on the calendar prior to the event execution. It starts with the money. You should have set a budget and a goal. How did you do staying inside the budget and meeting or exceeding your goal? In Chapter 9 – Buried Alive, there is specific guidance on how to conduct a post-event debrief.

This goes over who needs to be present, questions to ask, and how to ensure everyone's input.

Celebrate any level of success. Have a party at this debrief. Make some phone calls and shout out joy of success.

Segmented lists. Take time to learn your donor management system and identify different ways you can segment your donor lists. This will help you make the most out of your communications and solicitations. Here are some suggestions (this is by no means all inclusive):

- Gift amounts
- One-time donors
- Multi-year donors
- Event attendees

Hopefully, you have already developed many of these resources, and we are just talking about updating them. If you haven't, that is OK, too. However, the good part about these resources is that once you have them, you update them regularly, but you are not redoing them every year. Finally, some of these are plans you can create as you need them (many of these you need). The point here is that these are not long, elaborate narratives; they are more like recipes that you review when you want to make a favorite, impressive dish for a party. At some point, you will know them without having to look at the recipe. These plans, like any good dish, will always have people asking "how," so it is good to have them recorded in a brief and easy to follow format.

In Chapter 5, we talk about the importance of your donor management system and how valuable it is in understanding your activity model, guiding your skill development, and creating tools like segmented lists which will allow you to target your messaging.

✷ TOOLBOX ✷

Document your plan. If there is a formal plan or an informal plan, get something on paper so that you know what you have done and plan to do.

Track everything. You want to improve. That can be raising more money, helping more people, or several other things. The only way to know if you are improving is to track your progress. Choose what you want to monitor and track it. Be sure to involve those on the front lines on what you measure to ensure that some of what you track involves.

Data of Learning. What gets measured gets managed.

More than money. Your development plan is tied to the organization's mission. Play the "lottery game," and discuss what an increase in funds would mean to programs, staff, etc.

Identify other needed resources. Just like you document your plan, build the parts that support your plan. Resources like a stewardship plan, activity models, and event debriefs. (All of these are discussed in detailed in other chapters).

Chapter 5

The Right Equipment

You have been watching the commercials forever. You have done the math and with what you spend on your gym membership (that you don't use) each month, you could easily afford it. On the commercial, they say just thirteen minutes a day will make a difference. You can do fifteen minutes a day.

It has arrived. It gets set up in your room and that night you watch the DVD. For a couple weeks, you get up every morning and use the equipment for twenty minutes. You feel better, and your clothes fit better. You were right: This was so much better than having to leave and go to the gym.

You head to your reunion and get all the compliments you wanted. It was a wonderful weekend, a fun-filled weekend. Monday, it is back to the grindstone.

The alarm goes off, signaling you to get up and use the machine, but you are still exhausted from the fun-filled weekend. You will get back to your routine tomorrow. That night, one of the kids is sick, so you are tending to them. Then it is Wednesday. You never work out on Wednesday because you have your early morning sales meeting.

For the months leading up to your reunion, you did it every day. You were committed to using the new machine. Now you are using the machine infrequently (if at all). What happened? The kids use it more as entertainment (but they are getting exercise). The most common use for this great machine these days is as a clothes hanger.

This story is one we have heard or experienced before. It is also very similar to the story of a donor management system (DMS). Whether due to a conference or conversation with another development professional or a consultant's strategy, an organization acquires a software package to manage their donor relationships. Possibly, the system was acquired to address a specific need such as a campaign or a regular event; maybe it's for the function of specific personnel hires.

In the beginning, many people were involved in the implementation and initial training of the DMS. They all saw value in the new system. Over time, organizations are lucky if just one person still uses the system regularly. After that person leaves the organization, then what?

Like the piece of gym equipment that has more value as a clothes hanger, non-profits lose enthusiasm over their donor management systems, and they become transaction management systems that log donations and spit out acknowledgments and a few key reports.

These systems are powerful and capable tools that can help you increase your donor retention and organic gifts and impact your mission in many positive ways. In this chapter, we will discuss how to make these systems instrumental in your personal development and of your organization's development.

Modernizing Your Efforts

Many years ago (like in the 90s), I was in my manager's office, and we were training. We were talking about getting to know our partners, and he pulls out this "recipe box." He had two of these boxes on the corner of his desk—one black and one red. They were filled with 4x6 index cards. The black one was filled to the point that you probably could not fit any more in it and could not really close it. The red one was half full. Most of the 4x6 cards were dog-eared and had writing on both sides. Some of the index cards were even stapled together. On the top, in black marker, were company names. In the red box, some of the cards were brand new and had a little writing on only one side. Throughout both of the boxes, there were post-it notes sticking out with simple words like "call" or "B-day Wed."

My manager's boxes constituted what is affectionately called a "tickler file." The black box held his general relationships, and the red box held the "hot" or new relationships. Each week, he went through his tickler file and recorded notes about these relationships, making lists of activities or ways to grow these relationships (the post-it notes). In my naiveté, I was impressed with his organization and felt I could create a digital version. I would accomplish what his tickler file did along with creating an automatic alert of what his routine did with the press of a button or two.

No two people use the tickler file the same way. People learn tips and tricks from their predecessors and improve the process along the way. With customer relationship management (CRM) systems, there are best practices and fundamental truths, but no two people use it exactly same way. In choosing a CRM or donor relationship system, leadership learns how they can monitor activity and have information on *all* their donors in *one* place. This provides access to a bevy of *reports* versus having to go through individual tickler files.

We have come a long way from that earlier described "tickler file." These reports can communicate a lot of valuable information, but mostly, they can show leaders who is using the system and who is not. Like the tickler file, the more successful people in fundraising or other businesses are the ones who use the relationship management system. So before you become concerned about those reports, remember the alternative is the old tickler file system. There are lots of benefits to the digital system, including having someone else observe and utilize your activity. CRM benefits include the ability to share information about your donors, identify skill sets you can share with others, or identify skill sets you could use some help with. You can plan your workload and donor visits months out and pull a list of birthdays for your donors at the beginning of the month or the start of the week. Additionally, you will have the details of your last meeting easily available.

Choosing the Right System

I have a friend who is a doctor. I remember being together at an annual holiday get-together. He had some very descriptive words for the Internet and sites, such as WebMD, when all those online self-diagnosis sites began. We had a good relationship, so I carried on the conversation, and the result was advice that I have used throughout my career.

His complaint was that people went to the web researching the disease they thought they had and then (mistakenly) identified the symptoms they had based on their research. As a result, a lot of time was wasted because people created aches and pains based on what they read.

Instead, people should have written down the symptoms and then evaluated what they potentially had based on those symptoms. That way, they might receive the most impactful treatment and not a bunch of recommendations they don't need and that may cause more problems. Understanding symptoms, history, and needs is where most professionals begin.

How did I apply this to my work? When I begin working with a client, I start with what they currently have and why they need to change. If it were a car, I would ask about space, travel habits, and hobbies. That way, I could find them what they needed and some of what they wanted. It also made it easier when I needed to address the difference between their budgets and what they wanted.

When it comes to choosing the right donor management system for your organization, I provide the same advice. Whether we are talking about the organization's first system or changing to another system, start with where you are.

Answer These Questions:

What you currently do:
- What information do you currently collect on donors?
- What do you currently track on your donors?
- What is the process to review a donor's giving history?
- What is the process to acknowledge a donor?
- What reports do you need regularly (top donors, monthly contributions) and how do you compile these reports?

- How do you acquire online donations?
- How do you track interactions with donors?

To accomplish all that you do in fundraising, what other systems do you use:

- How is your accounting managed?
- How does your organization receive online contributions?
- What event management system do you use?
- What system do you use for email communication?
- What system do you use for social media management?
- If you have a system for peer-to-peer fundraising, who is it with?
- How do you prepare your acknowledgment letters?

About your current donor base:

- How many records are there from the last three years (at most)?
- How many people need access to donor information and transactions?
- Does there need to be different levels of access?
- Some other questions:
- What is your budget (see comments on expense)?
- Is there anything you are considering in your future development plan (peer-to-peer, auction, giving society)?

Managing the Expense

I have worked with organizations of multiple sizes and can confidently share that when used regularly, these systems pay for themselves in a short amount of time. Here are some ways DMS pay for themselves:

- Recapturing donors/improved donor retention
- Establishing reoccurring donations
- Accepting online contributions
- Creating time saved with single source system or centralization of information

As you evaluate the cost, be sure to consider not only the contract expense, but include some value for time saved in having a system that you will use. That is why you do everything you can to include everyone who will or should use the system, and make sure it is a system they will be excited about.

Identify the Right Features

The more data you can have centralized in one system, the more knowledgeable you and your organization will be. This equates to fewer steps while making sure you record donations and acknowledge donors. It also creates less opportunity for mistakes in recording the information due to it being a single system that generates reports, acknowledgments, tax information, and so on.

Payment Processor

Many of these systems allow you to process payments for your contributions. This allows you to have a secure payment system. These systems operate outside of your donor management system. This means you do not maintain any financial information (credit card or bank information) in your system. These systems often have negotiated special non-profit rates with the credit card companies.

Online Fundraising

If your system works with a payment processor, these programs often have tools so you can add a donation tool to your website. These tools allow people to immediately be updated or added in your central donor system, rather than making a donation through PayPal, or something similar, and having to add it to your donor system. This again alleviates extra steps.

Event Management

Events are involved and there are many details to manage. Add on top of that managing attendee information and ensuring that you capture the necessary information for future interaction. In addition to the hours spent on decorations, there is now the additional time spent on updating the information on donors.

If there is a part of your donor management that includes event management, then your donors will be able to update their own information. Also, another convenience is that you will have all the information for this event in one location.

Get a Demo

The majority of these systems are cloud-based. Most of these companies can set up demonstrations and training sites. Before you choose a system, take it for a "test drive." Complete standard activities; such as, adding a donor, setting up an acknowledgment letter, and adding a contribution. You should test the system in every way you use your current system(s). If there is a third-party system you use regularly, ask if this system provides a similar service, including event or email management. Can your current system integrate with this system? Test this integration to ensure information populates correctly.

If you can complete a regular function (adding donors and contributions, pulling reports) with minimal instruction, then you have a system you can use. If using the instructional videos answers the questions you have, then this is a system you will use. Whether or not you will use a specific donor management system depends primarily on your commitment to learn the system. Ease of use is 50 percent the result of using the new system and 50 percent the design of the program. As a person that has used no less than twenty different customer relationship management systems, I can say there is a large spread in user friendliness between programs.

If they cannot set up a trial system for you to "play with," then ask for current users in your area. Ask to meet with them and observe them using the system. We are not talking about a daylong shadow but more of a one- to two-hour meeting where you communicate specific things you want to witness. Here is an agenda of activities you might want to observe:

- Adding a donor
- Entering a donation
- Generating an acknowledgment
- Pulling an event report
- Pulling monthly donations over $200
- Asking who uses the system regularly

Prepare the Information

Whether you are changing software or getting your database set up for the first time, this is an opportune time to go through your data and clean it up. When deciding what data needs to go into your new donor management system, I would suggest you limit your data to the last three years. You want your most current and active donors. Many of the cloud-based systems charge you based on the number of records. You do not want wasted space and expense just because someone made a single gift six years ago.

If this is the first time setting up your DMS, you may have several separate sources with the same information (i.e., donor names from campaigns, events, and volunteers). Many systems require you to upload information in a format that is called comma separated values (.csv). It would be valuable to organize your data so it is consistent (same headers) from each source. This will make it easier for the new system to identify duplicates. You often need to upload donor information and transaction information separately.

Prior to uploading your data, sort it by address, then by name. You may also find some duplicates or additional members in a single household. When doing this, you may discover a single individual with multiple records that you could miss. For example, you may have an individual listed:

- *John Doe*
- *Jack Doe*
- *J.L. Doe*

At the same time, you may find multiple people in the same household. Many systems allow you to set up that relationship in the upload by adding a single column for those records that have other members. From an address sort, you may find the following listings.

- John Doe
- Jack Doe
- Jane Doe
- M.J. Doe

The more you can do to prepare your data, the better and more reliable your data will be for future use. You will want to set up standards on data entry. This is a great help when you filter your data through other databases, including the National Change of Address Database. Suggestions would be deciding on directional labels like north and south, or how you communicate "apt." (apartment) or "ste." (suite) before a location number. For example, which of these two formats does your organization desire?

- 1001 North Main Street, Apt. 205
- 1001 N. Main St., #205

This is one of those times when an ounce of prevention is worth a pound of cure. The more you can do to make your data "clean," the more valuable the information that comes from your donor management system will be.

Once you upload your donor data, the system assigns a constituent number. To help your transactions match appropriately, consider using the new donor ID number with each transaction.

Many software companies will offer to clean your data and manage your upload to their system. If it is a flat fee, then it is probably worth it. Cleaning your data is often labor intensive and is done regularly by these companies. The companies can advise your organization about your raw data.

Consider the Outcomes

In addition, share reports you regularly generate from your donor management system. If these are reports that you create based on multiple reports you generate currently, I would share with the software company to see if they can develop an automated and concise report that includes the information you typically gather. These could be reports you generate for board meetings, leadership, or audits.

Also, consider custom information you may want to add to your donor profiles. It could be how you acquired the donor, the donor's relationship to the organization, or participation in a giving society. Custom fields could be some of the ways in which you want to segment donors or particular groups of people that you want to pull select information on. This could be set up with the information you upload or done immediately after the upload.

This is also important in choosing the correct system for your organization. If it is more difficult for you to get the information you regularly use, you are not getting a better system. There are many good donor management systems, and I have found the information at Capterra to provide good guidance. I really value the live reporting feature available on Bloomerang. In their reporting feature, one can design the report they want on the screen and see how the information is delivered. However, their donation forms are a little less aesthetic than those at Salsa or Network For Good .

Whatever system you choose, take time to find a local organization that is using it, and sit with someone to see what they like about it and also improve about it.

⚒ TOOLBOX ⚒

Choosing a DMS can propel your organization to the next level. This is only true if it is one you will use. Here is a summary of ways to ensure that this is the best system for you:

- Be clear on what you do now
    - How many different systems do you use
    - How many steps is there in recording a donation and generating an acknowledgment
- Get a demo—see if they can set up a trial system that you can test using the system
- Talk to current users—ask for names of current users from the sales rep
- Consider outcomes
- Ask: What reports do you need to generate?
- Ask: What groups do you want specific info about?

⚒

CHAPTER 6

THE RIGHT STRATEGY

You jumped on the scale this morning, and you haven't lost a pound. You have been working so hard . . . or so you thought. You look back at the app that monitors your activity, and it hits you. Only one day above 15,000 steps (your average for the week is 8100 steps). You drank more coffee and soda than water this week, too. Every day, these annoying little devices monitor our activity and require us to look in the mirror when we don't get the results we want. The goal could be losing weight or maintaining fitness. When you gain weight, it is a wake up call. You frantically respond by drinking more water, starving yourself a little, parking a little farther away, or taking the stairs. We know what is needed to accomplish our goals.

A DMS can be just as annoying as those fitness trackers we put on our wrist. Unlike the fitness trackers, DMS do not automatically record your activity. Yet, when your organization is facing a decline in contributions, you are forced to take the same hard look in the mirror. If you are not updating your system regularly, then you don't have the same eureka moments. When you don't lose weight or dare we say, gain a little, it can be explained as you monitor your step count. Likewise, when contributions are down, it could be because you are not connecting with donors. If you are not logging your donor engagement, the cause may not be apparent. How do you know how to react?

Donor management systems are amazing tools. When used well and consistently, you will be aware of your revenue from contributions. There are very few surprises. This chapter gives you helpful hints on how to make the most out of these systems.

The success of these systems comes with setting them up to be a part of your plan. In Chapter 4, we discussed the importance of tracking everything. This includes: the funds raised on a monthly basis, your face-to-face engagements with donors, response to events and activities, and many other factors that can be logged and tracked.

Start With the End

Figure out what you want to accomplish in your development efforts. This will help you identify what you want to track. Think about what questions you have when you look at your annual contributions.

- What segments of donors do you want to know about (board, staff, alumni, giving society members, etc.)?
- What information do you need to add to your donor profiles (email, employment, volunteer interests, birthdays)?
- What campaigns do you have planned (growth, capital, new programs)?

Use "Custom" Fields

You have discerned the information you want at the end of the year; now make it easy to gather this information. Most DMS have the opportunity to add "custom fields" to the system. These fields will help you to pull out information you know you want in an easier way.

A custom field may be "Donor Groups," allowing you to select where people should be included. A donor group designation could be your staff, board, or giving society members. Other suggested fields may be program interests, such as children, environment, and financial stability.

You may want to identify those who give monthly. By adding this custom field, you can search by this field rather than trying to remember how to query for donors who give multiple gifts a year.

Many schools include information, such as the year alumni donors graduated. Are there graduates or participants in special programs that you want to track?

Decide on Your Metrics and Set Goals

Donor relationship management systems can track a great deal. You can track face-to-face engagements, phone calls, notes, contributions, and more. Take time to figure out what activity is most valuable for you to track. Also understand why you chose to track a piece of information.

Because strengthening relationships is important in donor management and growth in contributions, there is value in face-to-face engagements. One metric you may want to watch is the number of face-to-face engagements in a week. To take it one step further, you may want to look at your appointment setting skills by tracking appointments for in-person engagements.

Other metrics to monitor may be general activity, like emails or personal notes. These are also called touches—ways to cultivate your relationships with donors.

Use the Tools in the System

Many of these data tracking systems have tools that make recording your interaction more convenient. For example, many of these systems have a BCC email address. When you include this BCC address in your emails to donors, it will automatically include the email in the donor's record.

Another feature is the ability to add "open" activities. These activities show up on your front screen and remind you to do things for a donor. For example, a donor may request a report during a meeting, and you set up an open activity in the future, reminding you to send the donor the report.

Many DMS also have mobile apps that offer abridged versions. You can immediately record conversations after a meeting, or before walking into a meeting, know when a donor last made a contribution.

Every Interaction Needs a Next Action

Every time you meet with a donor, of course you should log it. You should also schedule the next activity. More than just when there is a required follow-up, these next activities make sure you do not forget donors. We all know that we should be touching donors multiple times a year. Often, many of our mid-level donors (that are ripe to become major) are forgotten. By scheduling your next activity to occur within three to four months, you help retain that donor.

Through using these suggestions, you have your week planned and you are working pro-actively rather than reactively. Imagine walking in on Monday not having to figure out which donors you need to reach out to but having the list generated from your activity from the last several months.

This is planning goes beyond the thank you note or event follow-up. These are true touches about organizational impact and updates on the organization. Remind yourself to ask about the trip they were planning or the progress on the big work project.

Become Proactive

The more you use your Donor Management System, the more it will become a part of your routine and plan. These systems can provide a wealth of information for your development plan and an understanding of your revenue flow. Instead of your annual goal divided by twelve, why not look to your monthly DMS reports and set your goal based on what you recorded during the same month last year. This data can help you achieve and exceed your development plan's goals.

Another way to use your DMS is to get ahead of contributions. Pull a nine-month-out report (also called an anniversary report). This is a list of contributions that were given to you nine months ago or three months before the anniversary of those gifts. This allows you to ensure you have engaged these donors prior to making another ask or know if they have made additional contributions since the anniversary of this gift.

By knowing what significant gifts came in and having a plan to engage your donors, you can grow your contributions and increase donor retention. I have two great stories about this. The first one involves a donor who had regularly given a five-figure gift around tax time each year. The donor had just taken custody of his grandkids due to an unforeseen circumstance. Because we had set this meeting as a result of data from an anniversary report, we learned we would not get that significant gift; however, he did give us a credit card number to pull a $500 monthly gift.

The second story about pulling this report is when we saw a number of donors who gave in memory of a treasured volunteer. As a result, we made a phone call and visited with her husband. After paying our respects and reminiscing about her work with the organization, we talked about a special project at the organization. A week later, we received a $1000 check from the husband.

Another report you can pull is a list of your top donors. Take the time to make sure you are engaging these donors. By using the custom fields feature, perhaps you add a marker to these accounts that says, "TOP 50." If you do not have fifty significant donors, then develop your list. Add this marker to your top twenty or thirty donors and then add another twenty to thirty prospective donors to this marker. Then pull activity reports based on this marker to make sure you regularly engage these donors.

There are many other valuable pieces of data that are available in your systems. Consider what data may be valuable as you create your annual development plan. For instance: "pull last year's gala attendees reports." Why? That may seem like common sense, but when you are in the throws of event planning, these notes (which can make your life easier) can be forgotten. Make them a part of your checklist or planning calendar.

Create Accountability

Through the report features in a DMS, you can create custom reports. Most of them have many standard reports you will also need, such as LYBUNTY (last year but unfortunately not this year), gifts needing acknowledgments, or a myriad of other reports. However, most boards and leadership want some unique set of information. Again, the more you use this system, the more you will find information from these systems helps you move your contributions forward.

One way to proactively move forward is to create a worksheet that can be used to create accountability for your development program. This worksheet could include information like the number of face-to-face engagements, number of appointments, contributions received, pending ASKS, plans for upcoming events and help needed, and other comments that can inform others of your status or needs.

DEVELOPMENT STAFF WEEKLY WORKSHEET

Staff Member Name _____   Date _____

Fiscal Year Start _____
Fiscal Year Week _____

Annaul Goal _____
Goal To Date _____ ((Annual Goal/52)xFiscal Year Week)

Amount Raised _____

Asks to be pledged/ rec'd in next 30 Days				
Name	Date Made	Next Act Date	Amount	Details

New Asks planned in next 30 days				
Name	ASK Date	Last Act Date	Amount	Details

Activities

Total Activities	_____
Appt Sets	_____
Face-to-Face	_____
ASKS	$_____
Amount Rec'd	$_____

These worksheets should be a part of your annual plan and goals. For instance, part of the worksheet should indicate where you are in relation to those goals and the support you need to accomplish necessary donor engagement. Support including program information or budget needs.

Taking twenty minutes or less to review this worksheet regularly with an in-depth meeting (one hour max) once a month helps everyone stay informed and ahead of potential challenges. It's not always airtight—crisis do happen—but open communication flow and review can often overcome many challenges that arise.

Ask for Direction

My Protestant clients and friends remind me that nowhere in the Bible does it say, "God helps those who help themselves." However, a Benedictine priest and my grandmother would use this phrase often. That phrase may not be located in the Bible, but take a look at the parable of the three servants in Matthew 25:29. In this parable, the servants who used the talents given to them by the master to get more talents were rewarded. The parable concludes, "Those who use well what they were given, even more will be given."

As I have shared: These systems are powerful and complex. You do not need to navigate your way through these systems by yourself. My clients consider me an expert on these systems, but I will share a little secret. I am an avid user of their help systems. These systems are multi-layered. Many of them have short videos (no more than fifteen minutes each) that show you how to use specific features. If that is not enough, there are often user forums. These user forums address specific challenges or unique ways in which one organization may use a system in comparison to another.

Finally, DMS companies often have blogs and webinars that can prove helpful for your organization. Many of them share how their system-specific features can be integrated into a greater plan. In Chapter 3: Answering the Call, I shared that fundraisers can increase their annual results by an average of $37,000 by engaging in learning opportunities. The blogs and webinars provided through the companies of these programs are learning opportunities. Where they may not directly result in funds raised, they can return time or reduce redundant systems so that you and your organization are more efficient and productive.

⚒ TOOLBOX ⚒

Start with the end—Think about what information about your donor population you are always asked about or you wish you could easily access. Setup your donor profiles to make it easier to pull this information.

Identify your most used reports—If these are your most used reports, then they should be part of your plan.

Become proactive—When you track and monitor your activity you become aware of patterns. The patterns help you prepare for challenges, such as low contribution months, or ensure that you don't miss out on large annual contributions. Make these systems work for you rather then make using these systems more work.

Create a tool—Develop a tool that is used to communicate what is going on with your donors, one that can be reviewed regularly and stimulate discussion.

Get educated—Many of these systems have significant education tools, including webinars, blogs, and short videos. Engaging in just one hour a week can support your development as a professional.

CHAPTER 7

WHAT I LEARNED FROM WOODY, BUZZ, AND NEMO

O nce upon a time there was a confident cowboy. He was the group's favorite. More importantly, he was the owner's favorite. Every day he led the others. Then, one day, there was a new favorite, a space ranger. Because of the new member of the team, he had to share his role as favorite . . . or did he? Because he wasn't ready to share his owner or status, he created one challenge after another. And because of a challenge gone wrong, he needed the help of the space ranger. Until finally, they realized they were better as a team of favorites, and the cowboy and space ranger became best friends.

Do you recognize the story? If you guessed *Toy Story*, you're right! The above story is placed in a format called the Pixar storyboard. If you were to search the term "Pixar storyboard," you would get something that looks like this:

Once upon a time, _____.

Every day, _____.

One day, _____.

Because of that, _____,

and because of that, _____.

Until finally, _____.

This is a great format to use to put together stories that explain the impact of your organization. I believe we, those in the non-profit world, can learn a great deal from the for-profit world. Pixar is an example of those for-profit businesses.

On the blog, "Studiobinder," Mary Risk shares details of the Pixar storytelling formula and why it works. As it relates to non-profits, the article talks about embracing emotion. In one section, she talks about emotions as adult themes. The article further explains you can't do emotion without teaching a lesson. Emotion is part that makes any story compelling. Your best story is not about the mass numbers of people you have helped, but the individual for which your organization truly made a difference. Emotion is rarely explained; it is witnessed. Emotion is the joy on a child's face when they get a new toy or enjoy their favorite meal. Emotion is the quivering lip or the frown when someone remembers a loved one through a photo, a favorite song, or a shared memory. Pixar does an amazing job of allowing us to witness emotion. If you were to watch the first fifteen minutes of the Pixar movie, "*UP!*," you'd discover, there are no words, just shared experiences and moving music.

Next, Ms. Risk explains how Pixar does a great job of living in the "grey." Is Woody of *Toy Story* the villain because he tries to get rid of Buzz? Is the Waternoose, the owner of the scream factory in *Monsters, Inc.*, evil because he was trying to figure out another way to capture scares? The villains and the good guys are not always clear. That is why the Pixar stories resonate with so many.

Storytelling is Our Marketing

Storytelling is our marketing in the non-profit industry. Today, storytelling is really now a form of marketing in every industry. I am not talking about "stories" that are present for twenty-four hours on Facebook and Instagram but stories that drive response. Think about the stories that are created around the holiday season, from the funny Coca-Cola bears sharing a soda and a smile, to the little kid chasing a remote control car that pops from under the tree and leads to a returning parent that has been deployed as a member of the military.

I am not talking about Uncle Charlie's stories that go on forever and make half the room uncomfortable. I am talking about stories that drive emotion and have a call to action.

In today's world, these stories need to be clear and concise and defined inside two minutes. This is why the format of the Pixar storyboard is so helpful. As we discuss further in this chapter, our donors and supporters, like many consumers, act emotionally and justify logically. Storytelling in marketing encourages the emotional connection with our organization.

Where statistics are often important to our story, they shouldn't be the only story or the majority of the story. Again, **people act emotionally and justify logically**. Statistics are important in justifying the initial gift and can be important in securing a second gift.

Identify your Starfish

There was a man walking down a beach covered with starfish that had washed up. As he continued down the beach, he came across a small boy who was picking up one of the hundreds that had washed ashore. The man asked the boy what he was doing. The boy eagerly responded, "Saving the starfish!"

The man said pessimistically, "You can never save them all, and tomorrow more will wash ashore. You won't make a difference."

The boy picked up another starfish, and calmly explained, "To this one, I am making a difference."

Josef Stalin said it best when he explained, "That one is a tragedy; many are a statistic."

I often receive solicitations that use statistics to explain the impact of the organization. From the pounds of food they distribute, number of lives saved, number of children educated, what a dollar can accomplish, and many, many other statistics.

What is missing in these marketing pieces is the story that I can connect with. The funny and moving story about a child that reminds me of my child, my niece, or the cute kid in my neighborhood. The struggling person who shares characteristics with someone I know. The struggling person who could very easily have been me with one wrong decision. When this connection happens with a donor, it is called transference.

Stories allow donors to better understand what your organization does and the difference that your organization makes. Even when you do a great job sharing your story and explaining the impact of the organization, you still will not connect with everyone. To use the metaphor of the starfish, instead of connecting with the starfish being returned to the water, there will be some potential donors who connect better with concept of finally making it to the shore and discovering someone who cares.

It is About People and Relationships

The more universal you can make the situation, the more donors are likely to connect. How generic can you make the protagonist so that people can relate to them?

A perfect example is Matthew McConaughey's character in the movie based on John Grisham's best-selling book, *A Time to Kill*. In his closing arguments to the jury, he described the poor beaten body of a ten-year-old girl. He asked the jury members to close their eyes and then painted a very detailed picture that was hard for anyone to imagine, but one that even made him emotional describing it. Up until his last sentence of his closing argument, even though what he described could have been any ten-year-old little girl, it was clear to all it was the daughter of the Black defendant. Then he says, "Can you see her? Now, imagine she's white."

At that, he chokes back tears, and you see a jurist's mouth drop open and other members of the jury with tears streaming down their faces. This is what is called transference.

Transference is when the storyteller helps the listener replace the protagonist with someone they can relate to—whether themselves, a family member, or a close friend. By focusing on the situation rather than the demographics and environment, you make the protagonists more relatable.

Matthew McConaughey's character draws the line for this all-white jury with a simple phrase: "Imagine she's white." Drawing those lines for a donor is imperative to helping her understand the impact of her gift. Transference happens when you connect through emotion.

Another industry we can learn from is performing arts. One of the tenants of the theatre is, "If you want to make an audience cry, you must first make them laugh." Life is often a roller coaster of emotions, and the best stories are the ones that imitate life. Think about the mother, who one day is celebrating her child's list of firsts and achievements (first steps, first words, first catch, first trophy), and the next day, she's worried sick as she sits next to her child in a hospital bed.

Through transference, or what I call the "statistic of one," it is no longer about just doing good in the community, it is about making a difference for someone you know and having an impact the donor sees and can relate to.

Transference is the ability to see yourself or someone close to you as the protagonist. It is when you recognize the universality of the situation. It is about focusing on the life of the person who is impacted. If it is a person living with disease, it is about the routine of his day. If it is a child facing hunger, it is about the child being fed enough so they thrive at school. If it is a developing village, it is about the woman who is the strength and glue that holds the family together. More than discussing the demographics of the environment, you focus on the individual's situation. William Shakespeare offers timeless examples in his storytelling, including the excitement of forbidden love in *Romeo & Juliet*, or the difficulty of having siblings in *Taming of the Shrew.*

By adding a name to a story (whether it is the real name or not), the person telling the story helps people connect with a living entity they can relate to. For example:

Please give to help sheltering needs this winter.

Karl, a local vet, will not survive the evening without your help, especially if the temperatures get below freezing. Please give. It's just nine dollars for one night in a shelter.

In my work with addiction and recovery centers, the most powerful statistic I heard is that one in three households are impacted by addiction. The concept of "street corner deals" is no longer a way to describe today's addicts. More often, they are soccer moms, hard-working breadwinners, or successful individuals who have become addicted as a result of an injury or trying to remain competitive and working beyond normal human capacity. The majority of addicts I met through these clients could have been one of my friends. It could have been me after one bad decision. That was the transference needed to discuss the organizational need to donors.

Can't Stop Telling It.

If you have a really great mission (I know you do) and an amazing testimony, the mission's story is universal. Meaning, when you craft the right story to explain your mission, it is a story you should be telling next week or a great story that you can pull from the archives ten years from now to share.

I have many stories like that.

A mother came home from volunteering for meals on wheels to find fire trucks putting a fire out at her house. As she scanned the situation, she saw her child's mattress on the front lawn with his favorite cartoon sheets on it. Overwhelmed by the situation, she passed out.

When she came to, she was sitting in the van with a disaster volunteer and the AC blowing. Mr. Bill reassured her that no one was hurt. The principals were on the way with the kids, they had a hotel room to go to for the next few days, and he was there to help.

Sometimes, being able to add updates to these stories are as powerful as the stories themselves. For instance, another story I learned *was about a man who was a successful regional manager who was holding on by a string trying to hide his addiction. For some reason, he went into a church and heard the testimonies of a faith-based addiction and recovery organization.*

After hitting rock bottom, he enrolled in that organization, and it literally saved his life. After graduating from the program, he took the opportunity to live in their aftercare program. He saved money and found a worthwhile job and got back on his feet.

The update: He got married, had a beautiful child, and is now making a difference in the lives of other addicts as a staff member in a way that only one who has experienced addiction can.

Stories Can Be Told in Many Forms

Successful storytelling allows for a story to be shared in multiple forms. The oral and written history is the most common, and it helps to have the template of the Pixar storyboard until you get more comfortable retelling stories.

Eventually, it is beneficial if the story can be shared in multiple formats. Is there a single quote contained in the story that can get people interested in the "rest of the story" as Paul Harvey, one of radio's greatest storytellers, would say. This is where social media is powerful in sharing memes or snip-its from videos.

If we were to pull from the two stories referenced above of the fire victim and the addict and put together these images and pull quotes, it might lead others to be curious.

For the fire victim—a picture of a smoldering mattress with this quote: "I saw my son's mattress on the front lawn and could not recall where my children were . . . Mr. Bill let me know everything was going to be okay."

For the addict—a picture of the entrance to the center with this quote: "It was divine intervention that caused me to walk through those doors. That day, my life changed!"

In addition, short videos can share testimonies that make an impact. The goal is to get as much out of one testimony as possible. This repetitive message is not just a recommendation when it comes to successful marketing, it is a rule.

The Rule of Seven is a real marketing rule. This rule says that it takes seven times of seeing or hearing a message for one to act on it. When the community sees a repeated image or story, they will associate it with your organization. When supported by local news or human-interest stories, they will better understand your impact. If you always include giving guidance with your story, people will look for ways to recognize your impact.

It Takes Everyone's Effort

This is where the culture of philanthropy can be a part of your organization. The more people you can involve in collecting mission-focused stories, the better chance you will have to craft stories that connect with different donors. Empowering others in the organization to collect photos and testimonies or names of clients who are willing to share their appreciation for the organization can be an invaluable asset. This is something that every staff members can do as part of fundraising.

Setting up a collection bank on a shared drive is one way you can do this. Another way is to set up a recognition program to acknowledge the efforts of those who help with these activities. For instance, you could give away movie tickets or $5 gift cards to individuals who connect you with moving stories. The value in this activity is the greater opportunity to capture important stories.

Great stories are the stories that get told and re-told by anyone and everyone, and the story is timeless—always relevant. Example of these types of stories would be forbidden love of star-crossed teenagers as described by William Shakespeare; or it could be the change of heart of a lonely miser that found companionship in gold but discovered the reward that comes from giving, as shared by Charles Dickens; or it could be the unlikely friendship of a cowboy and a space ranger. When these stories are solid, they easily roll into other mediums, such as theatre or movies or songs. How many times have you heard the tune or the words to that famous song from *Toy Story*, "You've Got a Friend in me?"

The focus here is not necessarily on getting the largest contribution but more on getting the first donation and working a good stewardship plan (see our introduction to stewardship plans in Chapter 4 or continue to building relationships in the next chapter).

✕ TOOLBOX ✕

Organize your Stories—The Pixar storyboard is a great format to organize a standard way in which you tell your stories. Having this format will allow you to recall any testimony and retell it in a clear and concise manner.

Get Help—This is a great way to build the culture of philanthropy. Involving members of your team who are involved with direct delivery of your mission can help collect testimonies and pictures that can connect donors with the organizational impact.

Build a Story Bank—This has two aspects. First, set up a shared drive that allows others in the organization to deposit pictures and client testimonies. Then create a place where leadership can find the compelling stories that demonstrate the impact of your organization.

Check out the definitions section at the back of this book for more information.

Chapter 8

Who Really Matters

One time, when I was seven or eight years old, my father took me to work with him on his day off. On the way, we stopped at my favorite place, McDonald's. I got my favorite hotcakes, and Dad got two egg McMuffins. Two egg McMuffins? When we got to the office, my father gave one of his McMuffins to the guard on duty. I sat with that guard and smothered my hotcakes with syrup. We spoke about lots of things, but he made sure to tell me, "You have a great dad!" A few minutes later, my dad returned with some files, enjoyed his McMuffin with us, and we left.

My father found value in everyone, from the custodian to the CEO. He would often tell me that surrounding yourself with the right people always made life better, not easier—not smoother, just better. Relationships won't take away the burden, pain, or struggles. They will give you a shoulder to lean on, maybe someone to lighten the load, and someone to lend an ear and encourage you.

Success in fundraising comes from the ability to manage relationships. We all have different roles in our personal lives when it comes to relationships. It should be no different in the fundraising world. In fundraising, we call it segmentation. Instead of designating it family, close friends, work friends, and acquaintances, we identify these relationships as major donors, event attendees, sponsors, and so forth.

In our personal lives, when there are people we want to get to know beyond the cordial handshake or a "like" on Facebook, we inquire and make time to get to know them. This isn't everyone you meet, just the people who have interests or values we have identified as those we can connect with. It may be a feeling they will challenge us in a unique way. It could be something they said that made you believe, "This is someone I would enjoy spending time with." An obvious connection, like the enjoyment of a sport or a specific sports team or the shared interest in a hobby could motivate further interaction. In our personal lives, some would call this courting. According to Webster's, courting is the act of paying special attention to someone in order to win their support or favor.

In fundraising, we identify this as cultivation: the act of moving someone from a place of interest to making a donation or a more significant contribution. After someone has donated, working on the relationship with a donor is called stewardship.

The Relationship Triangle

When I was leading sales teams, I learned about the relationship triangle. In order to close a sale, you had to close the triangle. Closing the triangle meant that all the parties were connected: the representative, the buyer, and the product being represented. It was also the key to a long-term sale. There is no difference when we are talking about the donors.

The State University of New York in Albany conducted research years ago, which demonstrated that the number one reason people donate is because someone asked. That fact is often what is forgotten. People think that just because they tell everyone about the organization and its mission and explain the need, people will be motivated to give. Rather than hope that someone will give, it is better to have asked. In this situation, you only have two legs of the triangle: a relationship between the representative and the donor and then the representative and the organization that is being represented.

The other reason why people give is because they have witnessed or have received direct benefit from the organization. For instance, perhaps during a disaster, they received sheltering from the American Red Cross. In this situation, again there are two legs of the triangle initially built. There is a connection between the organization and the donor and the person who receives the donation also has a relationship with the organization. In fundraising, the three legs become: the Fundraising rep, the donor, and the mission.

Through cultivation and stewardship, the opportunity to build the third leg is created. In the first scenario illustrated below, the organization can build a relationship through using the existing relationship. Through engaging the donor directly, the organization can build value in its mission. Regularly sharing stories about the impact of the organization through testimonies helps donors visualize the impact. Often, donors can exchange the names or faces of the testimonies with people they know who have had similar challenges. It could be a child who had a similar medical challenge or a family member that has faced the demon of addiction. This transference allows the donor to connect with the organization.

In the second scenario, a representative has the opportunity to build a relationship with the donor. It is not always possible to engage every donor, but having engagement and a stewardship plan will help you reach many. Each time the donor has the opportunity to engage with a person, you build that third leg.

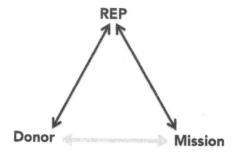

Scenario 1

Scenario 2

Donors can be engaged through a handwritten note or an invitation to volunteer with the organization. A personal invitation to an event lets a donor know that you are interested in him, especially if you can share why you feel this would be a good event for him to attend.

Multiple Relationships are Better

There was a father with many sons, and they often quarreled amongst each other. He brought them together and handed them a bundle of sticks. As the bundle was passed from one son to the other, he asked them to break the bundle. No one could.

Then he handed the sons a single stick from the bundle and asked them to break it, which they did with ease. The father then pointed out the difficulty they had in breaking the bundle when all the sticks were together. You are stronger together. That is the value of relationships—when you work together, for a common cause, it is harder for outside influences to break you.

Unfortunately, the average tenure for a fundraising professional with a single organization is between eighteen and twenty-one months. Some fundraising professionals take a book of business or a list of donors with them. As a result, they often get accused of stealing donors from one organization and taking them to another.

Here is the truth: Your development person probably tried to get leadership and the board involved in engaging significant donors multiple times. It could have been by suggesting a board thank-a-thon. Possibly, he or she requested that leadership make a phone call or write a personal note to share the organization's appreciation. Even to request a personal invitation to an event or a tour. For whatever reason, these activities did not occur, and the only time the donor heard from the organization (outside of contact with your fundraising professional) was to ask for money. Therefore, the donor felt like the organization did not care for them, except as an ATM. When the fundraising professional relocated, and their new organization needed some help, they were contacting someone they had a personal relationship with and would understand if they could not or would not support the mission of the new organization. However, because it was someone they knew who asked, there is a high probability they would make some sort of contribution. The organization had only one stick (the fundraiser) rather than a bundle (fundraiser, leadership, and board), and the easily relationship broke.

At best, current donors are supporting another valuable organization in the community. At worst, they shift their support from one organization to another. This is most likely because they have no other relationships with the organization. Think about the research I shared early or the scenarios of the relationship triangle. Was the triangle closed? Were any of the legs of the triangle strengthened, as the father in the story above did by adding sticks to the bundle?

In larger organizations, I have witnessed development staff acting very possessive of donors they have relationships with. It is valuable to the organization that every donor has multiple people with whom they feel comfortable connecting. To the best of my knowledge, it is against the code of ethics for a fundraising professional to receive commission on any donation; therefore, there is no need to be possessive.

Team Fundraising

On my sales team, I had two outstanding people. Part of what made them outstanding was their ability to work together and match one person's strength to the other person's weakness. Terry and Christine certainly did. Terry was exceptional at the inquiry and understanding a client's needs and motivation. Christine was exceptional at using impact statements to build value and was able to "bottom-line it," using the client's words. They each presented clear expectations of what would happen next to prevent client misconceptions or misunderstandings. Together, they MAXIMIZED their success.

Terry and Christine did not go on every client call together. They were each other's coach and cheerleader. They also kept each other focused and recognized when the other was not right for the client or the client was not right for them. This began because they were paired in role-play and peer training based on their complimentary strengths. Terry and Christine realized that they weren't competing with each other; they were working to improve their lifestyle. In addition, working together made their jobs fun and that was apparent to clients. Clients and donors like to work with "fun" people.

Internal Relationships Matter

Professional fundraisers are competing to achieve their missions and change lives. Not to mention, with the challenges we witness throughout our organizations, we need to have fun. *Relationships within our organization are just as important as the relationships we have outside of our organization.*

Speaking of internal relationships, here are a few ideas to help you recognize those who support your role in development. Team recognition is just as important as donor recognition. Don't forget to do either:

- Find ALL the bright spots—Because revenue generation is your role as the part of development, it is natural to get excited about the four-and five-digit gifts. But your team does not only have major gift officers with several years of experience. Make just as big a deal about your data person who has reduced your bad emails by 25 percent. Hum "Ode to Joy" because your coordinator found a new band for the special event. Don't forget the volunteer who was the first one to ask the HVAC company if they were supporters and now your new MGO got their first giving society member.

- Be Human—You are not the Pope and your thoughts are not infallible, nor are your ideas always the best. Be willing to adjust your plans based on input from your team. Welcome (and use) other people's ideas and give them credit. If you put a bad idea in place and get that feedback, admit your mistake.

- It is more than $$$—Money is a nice incentive for team members, but is least effective because most often it goes toward bills and necessities. There are plenty of other things available to you that will get you better results. For example, time off. Give away "off the books" half days. Stock up on "guilty pleasure" gift cards to McDonalds, Starbucks, and Cold Stone for some instant gratification. ***DO NOT*** under estimate the value of a handwritten *Thank You* note for a job well done.

- Make it Fun—Potlucks build a sense of family. Random dancing gives everyone the giggles. Crayons inspire creativity so make the next birthday card instead of buying one.

If the people around you feel valued and like you as a person and a member of their team, success happens.

It really does take a village. It takes everyone in your organization to be willing to leverage a relationship. Fundraising is hard, and it takes everyone being aware to make the connection and provide opportunities for fundraising. Even though program people or volunteers often are not asking for money or even trying to ask for money, to them, directing someone to the development staff is almost as bad as asking someone for money. This can be due to misperceptions of fundraising staff as used car salespeople rather than frontline customer service managers.

Therefore, value your internal relationships and steward them as you would your donor relationships. It is important the people on your team know, trust, and like you. Fundraising needs to be part of the culture. When a member of the team shares a story about an impacted life, it is the start of fundraising. When a front desk volunteer greets visitors and vendors with a smile and shares a program flyer, it is the start of fundraising.

Leadership needs to drive, encourage, and recognize this behavior called "building a culture of philanthropy." Public praise for bringing on a new donor or corporate partner always works well. Leadership inviting both program and development staff to lunch to build awareness and understanding of each side is effective. Fundraisers who pick up favorite beverages for office staff also helps. If you are the head development person, and you are working on a summer push, get discount movie theatre passes for non-development people and hand them out regularly and randomly. Everyone enjoys a summer blockbuster. A few dollars on internal recognition could drive thousands in organization revenue.

Know Thy Donor

It is often easier to get to know the people inside our office or environment since we see them every day. We need to work a little harder to connect with people who are not inside our purview on a daily or weekly basis. That is the value of reminders in Donor Management systems (as we discussed in Chapter 5).

In today's constantly changing world, we need to be adaptable and meet donors where they are. A famous meme says, "Success begins outside your comfort zone." For me, there was no truer statement the first time I almost completely interacted with a donor via Facebook messenger. I met this person at a Rotary meeting. They "friended" me on Facebook, and the interaction began and was almost completed on Facebook messenger. If it was not for an opportunity for the person to witness the program and its impact, I quite possibly could have secured a donation through a completely virtual process.

Social media has changed a great deal in our industry. As with many new things, social media doesn't replace traditional forms of engagement but is an additional form of engagement with which you need to become familiar. Most of what you need to "connect" with someone is on Facebook, LinkedIn, Twitter, or some other app. This still does not change the things that define what we, as professionals, do. Just like when email was added to direct mail or texting was added to cell phones, we simply have more tools in our box.

What is still paramount and necessary? It is still paramount to connect with your people, helping them move toward becoming stakeholders or remaining stakeholders. This includes connecting virtually through social media and other sources, as well as personably through notes and visits.

This is primarily managed through two primary strategies: cultivation and stewardship.

Cultivation is working with a prospective or current donor to build value and understand the impact of your organization. Cultivation can be done through sharing stories online, providing opportunities to engage with the mission of your organization, or through a conversation.

Stewardship is working with current, significant donors to help them understand their roles in your organization and the impacts of their gifts. As a professional, you should understand how donors choose to interact with you and the organization (notice I did not say *how you choose* to interact with the donors). Most likely, interactions involve multiple available tools.

In addition to social media, tools like Google Alerts can assist you with staying informed and provide talking points if needed. You can use these to watch for key information about specific donors or trends in your industry. Information will be delivered to your inbox only when information is added to the web. All you must do is choose the right key words, such as "Bob Smith, Acme Corp" or "House Fire, Gloucester." This is the evolution of reading the daily newspaper.

Another valuable tool involved in understanding our donors is the ability to inquire. Instead of telling a donor everything we learned about them from stalking their social media, give them the chance to share by asking questions and listening.

The ability to question is a skill, and it's like any skill that needs to be developed. It is also necessary to start any relationship. Think about an interview for a job: It is filled with questions. The strongest candidates are the ones prepared with questions of their own. Consider a first date: It is a volley of questions within conversation to consider if there is mutual interest for a second date. Many charitable organizations equip their fundraisers with a bevy of statistics, moving stories, and a laundry list of needs when they send them to meet with donors (especially when it is their first meeting with said donor). Understanding that not all stories and statistics are meant for all donors, the best way to discover which one's will connect best is through good questions.

As much as we provide new fundraisers with information, stories, and dollar handles, we need to provide them starter questions. Just a few, including, "How did you first become involved with ABC charity?" or "What is your favorite program?" should do the trick. Then we must practice this exchange as we practice our storytelling. Using these questions and soliciting valuable responses need to be as conversational as lunch with a longtime acquaintance would be.

In addition, it takes understanding the difference between open-ended and closed-ended questions or the value of continuing questions with "really?" or "you don't say?" Most importantly it takes practice. No great player walks onto a court and becomes a champion without practice, nor is a speaker admired because they are unscripted or unrehearsed.

A few things you accomplish by focusing on questions:

- **Build trust and rapport.** Because the focus is on learning rather than making an "ask," it allows everyone to be a part of a new paradigm. In fact, share when you start your meeting or set the appointment expectation as at time to learn about each other, and there will be no discussion of gifts or contributions.
- **Understand a donor's motivation.** Find out why a donor supports your organization. Ask the "lottery" question. (If you won the lottery and could fix one social problem, what would that be?") Learn about their goals in philanthropy or life.
- **Learn about capacity.** Listen for key identifiers, such as second homes or annual vacations to exotic places. Learn about the other organizations they support and why. Also, how have they supported those other organizations (stocks, bequests, annual fund, capital campaign)?
- **Establish credibility.** You have already put your relationship at a unique place by being focused on your donor rather than "the ask." Now, cement the process by having a clear next action. That could be gathering information by a next date, arranging an appointment, or a dozen other actions. Whatever it is, accomplish it before you say you will.

Take the time to role-play donor meetings. If you don't have anyone in your office or other teammates, contact a colleague from another organization. This is also a great opportunity to engage and prepare your board members. Role-playing is a great way to engage with non-development staff and demonstrate what you do and can help you build those internal relationships.

There are a myriad of tools available for those of us focused on fundraising. Like any personal toolbox, we have our favorites; just don't ignore the newer versions or other timesaving tools that may require learning and practice. To do so may be the same as ignoring an entire group of potential supporters.

Understanding NO Means KNOW

When it comes to funders, it is not uncommon for your initial request to get rejected. When that happens, grab hold of that NO, and help the funder KNOW more about the organization, while getting to KNOW more about the funder and their funding focus.

Most funders receive more applications for funding than they can review. Like resumes for a job posting, the average review is just seconds. The exception is when someone is familiar with an applicant

In my experience, I have never had a funder not be willing to help. As a result, 55 percent of the time, the organization received funding from the follow-up. Here are some ideas on how to start and maintain that dialogue.

- *Get that one-on-one meeting.* Take a moment to call, email, and show up to get that meeting with the person who sent you the letter. They may have a good gatekeeper; however most times, they are not trying to avoid you.
- *Be present.* Most funders put on seminars or open houses or lunches. Make sure you and/or your organization is represented at these activities. Be present by asking questions, giving feedback, and networking at these events.
- *Include the funder.* If you are hosting a public event (especially if it is free), invite the funder. Sometimes, they will come—especially if the invitation is personal, and the event demonstrates impact of the organization.
- *Ask for feedback.* If you plan to apply, talk to the funder to see if your organization's potential request matches the funder's objectives. Find out if there is a particular program the funder's representative identifies as a match to funding objectives.

These are just a few ways to improve your chances with grant funders. This chapter is about forming relationships. In working with any funder, whether we are discussing a major donor or the representative from a major funder, forming a relationship is always important. It puts a face to your non-profit. Like the story of the brothers, the more faces you can put with your non-profit, the stronger the relationship can be. As many of us do, our funders create associations to remember people and non-profits. This could be the memorable bow-tie guy or the enthusiastic lady with the beautiful scarves. The point is to embrace your quirks and put the best face on your non-profit.

✄ TOOLBOX ✄

- Build a donor's relationship with the organization and multiple individuals
- Building relationships internally is as important as donor relationships
- Know your donors through all means possible (social media), but don't forget to ask them directly
- Use online tools like Google Alerts or birthdays on Facebook and LinkedIn
- Work on and practice your ability to question and listen to responses
- Role-play
- Invite funders to get to know your organization when they say NO

✄

Chapter 9

Buried Alive

As fundraising professionals, we often feel pulled in too many directions when it comes to events. Identifying sponsors, sending invitations, and marketing are all equally important. A single task can easily become overwhelming to the point you feel buried alive.

I wanted to locate a solid story about being buried alive to kick off this chapter. I Googled it and went down a rabbit hole. These are the titles that popped up in my search (literally):

- "5 terrifying true stories of people being buried alive"
- "25 bone-chilling stories of being buried alive to scar your life"

Terrifying and bone chilling are phrases that grab you. I wasted ninety minutes reading through these stories. Then another thirty minutes going back to re-read the stories to find an appropriate one. I was easily distracted and lost two important hours.

Too often, event planning, like the research for this chapter, can be hijacked by an insignificant task instead of activities that help us accomplish our mission. What do napkin colors have to do with starving children or one-hundred-year bone-chilling stories have to do with planning an event?

Maintain Perspective

Many people think events are the way to raise money for their organization.

Whether it is a gala, golf tournament, breakfast, fun run, or any other event that is called a fundraiser, it is a significant time commitment and risk. When compared with the time necessary to cultivate a donor for a significant gift—$10,000 or more—there is little comparison. So why do events? In most cases, it is because your organization has not discovered the value of a *major gifts strategy*. When you consider the hours in committee meetings, researching venues and menus, set up, and the actual event, there is a considerable amount of waste compared to truly engaging your donors.

Based on the previous paragraph, it seems hard to justify any event. There is value in conducting one or two significant events annually. Part of the reason for events is that it is in our human nature to want to gather people around something we are passionate about. Beyond the chance to be amongst others that share our passion, there is:

- The chance to spotlight our mission and tell our story
- The chance to explain our impact and value
- The chance to engage volunteers and involve our community
- Opportunity to tap in to marketing dollars versus philanthropic contributions
- Opportunity to get some positive press about your organization
- Opportunity to attract new supporters that may not discover your organization otherwise

I am sure there are more, but I believe those few justify the effort. Events are used to engage and attract people who we would most likely not be able to reach. That may be through attendance or the notoriety the event may achieve. However, an organization should not be dependent on events.

There are many ways to measure the success of an event. Make sure there is a plan to measure the success and evaluate the event. I have witnessed many events that have gone past their prime. It is okay to give an event a sabbatical or transfer an event to another organization or even have a grand finale.

Start with the End

Begin with a clear goal. Primarily, the goal is monetary, but it could include multiple sub-goals, such as metrics for attendees, sponsorships, or first-time attendees. All goals should be easily evaluated at the conclusion of the event. Ensure the mission of the organization is clear and present throughout the event.

To help motivate everyone, tie the goal to an aspect of the mission. How many meals or how many clients will be served as a result of hitting the goal? Is there a special project or new program that will be funded if you hit this goal? For those who are passionate about your mission, this will motivate them to participate in any way possible.

Other goals may include having a percentage of event attendees who are first time attendees. This is an opportunity to grow your donor population. Focusing on new attendees is only valuable if you have a unique plan to engage those first time attendees post-event—a plan focused on getting those new individuals to become involved in the organization.

Whatever your goal is, make sure there are systems in place to evaluate the value associated with the goal. Is there a way to track ticket sales, first time attendees, and surveys to inquire about further interest in the organization? Do not be frustrated because you had a goal but did not ensure you could evaluate your goal. Make sure everyone involved knows what is being tracked and how. That way, everyone will understand why systems and protocols are set up. For example, they can understand why there might be this question on the ticket form: "Is this your first time attending the event." Whatever your goal is, take a few minutes to ensure you correctly set up and are able to track the information you need.

Now that you have defined your goals, it is important to have a plan to evaluate your event and celebrate your success. As part of your event planning, establish a date for a post-event rally and debrief within five days after the event. This provides an opportunity to all those involved to discuss the event, share their thoughts, and celebrate the event's success.

Document

My mother taught me the value of good records. Long before the days of computers, my mother had many manual systems and processes. She maintained records from one year to the next, which helped her to "make it all look so easy." She knew who did what tasks well, who gave the big bucks, and who brought the most guests. Mom was always more successful the next year because she knew what worked the previous year (and what didn't).

I learned this early on. Our fundraiser for Scouts was selling fertilizer. I maintained my sales list from one year to the next and grew it, constantly updating it. Part of my motivation was always paying for my summer trips (summer camp, high adventure, and national events). I always accomplished this because I maintained good records, just as my mother taught me.

Those you involve in the event, from volunteers, vendors, and donors, should be included on the documentation. If this is the first year for the event, having a specific budget may not be reasonable as you are designing the event. Take time to track your expenses. This will help you establish a budget in the future.

If this is a regularly occurring event or there is an intention for it to be, take the time to document everything. Every time there is a task that is accomplished or needs to be accomplished, add it to the list of tasks for the event. Place when the task needs to be accomplished on a timeline leading up to the event.

Keep documentation central and accessible. Information should be reviewed and compiled by as many people as possible. A sample of such a task lists and documentation is available at fundraisingis.com/bookresources.

(NOTE: If you have volunteers that graciously donate items for the event but choose not to be reimbursed for the values, still include them in your documentation. That may be a key aspect to your event design and may be an expense in upcoming years. Failure to note expenses covered by volunteer/committee member donations may leave you with an inaccurate picture of what is required to put on an event or the true event results.)

Critically Assess Resources (People)

Before you take on an event, you need to be clear about what resources are available to you. What resources do you *have*? Events are not just thrown together (at least not good ones you plan to repeat). They take a significant amount of time (which requires people), money (which requires people), and planning (which requires people). What is the number one overlooked resource by organizations? *People*. This does not mean create a supersized committee; it means have sub-committees or engage third parties to support the execution of the event. Your core group needs to be strong and willing. It is not recommended that the core group be paid staff (the paid staff needs to be represented, though).

If you are attempting to replicate an event you have attended, be realistic with your expectations. Understand that if the previous event was making $50,000+ and happening for multiple years, they probably did not raise that amount the first year. Is it a large non-profit that has many staff members as opposed to your organization that has a handful of staff? Is their signature sponsor on their board? Do you have a potential signature sponsors on your board?

Be careful not to do an event because everyone else is doing events. Ensure you have the resources to put on an event that will enhance your organization and improve your presence in the community. The last thing you want is to take on an event that will distract you from carrying out the mission of the organization.

Events need to be paid for. The primary costs associated with an event should be secured prior to the start of the event. Hoping to break even the night of the event leaves too much to chance. Give someone or a few people the chance to have their names plastered everywhere (invitations, at the entrance, ads, etc.). The income from attendees of the event should go toward the mission, not the cost of the event.

Identify the most significant cost for the event, and identify a presenting sponsor that covers at least 125 percent of that line item. This is typically the cost of the food or the venue. Because this allows the sponsors to display their names and logos everywhere, companies can use marketing or advertising funds rather than philanthropic contributions, which is usually a larger pool of money.

If you make a formal ask at some point during the event, then you should not be selling tickets. Make sure people are aware there will be a formal ask during the event. If you do not inform them, people search for something to donate, unprepared or confused. This limits your contributions. It is valuable to have informed attendees that will bring a check or have thought about what size of contribution to make.

If this is a ticketed event, remember this is a fundraiser and follow this formula.

[The cost per person for food and drink] x 3 or 4 = Ticket Price

I doubt your goal is to raise as little as possible or have as many people at your event that can't afford the real value of the items on your silent auction. I believe you want people with capacity and desire, people who can give more to your organization. If you need to do a discounted ticket for a select group of people (i.e., organization volunteers), then do that. Your public price should follow the formula.

- The first multiple allows all attendees to pay their own way and cover the costs of food. Yes, you have gotten a sponsor to cover this cost, but still this makes sense. That is why we say three or four. Read on to the other multiples.
- The second multiple is for all those other ancillary costs like tables, linens, decorations, audio-visual needs, etc. Before you know it, all those little extras add up to being a lot of extra money.
- The third multiple is for the people and the time that have been invested in this event. Yes, they are mostly (or all) volunteers, but they are valuable. Just because volunteer time is complimentary for your

organization, it does not mean those don't offer value to your attendees. According to Independent Sector, the average value for a volunteer hour is $24.69. How many hours were given by volunteers to make this event great?

- The last multiple is the actual donation. The part that is attached to the mission and vision of your organization and is the value of the impact you are making in the community

For example, if your per-plate cost is $18, then your ticket price should be between $60– $75. Every attendee (workers, volunteers, and staff) should pay if there will be an expense for their presence. Many groups struggle with higher ticket prices because they want to ensure the dedicated volunteers and staff members attend. There are multiple ways to include volunteers and staff without charging them the same rate to be a part of the event. At a minimum, make sure they cover their meal. Many software packages offer ways to include discount codes. Be sure to include this as one of your must haves when evaluating event/donor management systems (see Chapter 5: The Right Equipment).

Mission is Clear and Present

Have you ever attended a "charity" event and wondered what the charity was? It was an amazing event, offered great music, hosted a wonderful silent auction, and created an up-beat atmosphere. If you want bigger donations the night of an event, those higher bids that exceed normal values, make sure people know why they are there. Show pictures, give people testimonies to read, have recipients of services present and interacting with guests. Tug at every heart string you can to demonstrate the value of the evening and your organization.

A lot of groups use amazing graphics to promote their events but forget to put the "why" in the promotion. They have truly branded the event and made it a destination point on the calendar. For every time you promote your keynote speaker or items at your auction, there should be something about your mission. The "why" would someone want to come to and support your event, and don't forget to include the impact they are making if they attend. This formula is 2:1. You should be talking about your mission twice as much as you promote your event. Engage people to learn more.

Remember, the value proposition of your event: It is raising money for a great cause. Make sure people understand what that cause is and see value in it. Great ways to include mission in your event is to have your clients or participants serve specific roles at your events. Allow them to be servers, auction helpers, or greeters at your registration table. Rather than hire a speaker, allow your successful clients to provide testimonials.

Prepare large posters that illustrate your mission and that can be used in addition to the event. Have a PowerPoint running throughout the event that shares stories, statistics, and images of your mission.

These are just a few ways you can include mission in your event.

Scripts, Rehearsals, and the Details

The details are the difference between a good event and a great event. I am not talking about things like the color of the napkins or five flowers versus three in the centerpiece. Those details are only important if they are absent. I'm referring to details, such as a well-planned program, nametags with correctly spelled names, and well-placed logos with relevant information about your mission are the ones that add value to your event, thus increasing contributions.

Let's begin with the flow of your evening. When your event includes speakers and performances and presentations, they need to be scripted and rehearsed. Consider this: Your committee has planned every aspect of the evening to make sure it is the best representation of your organization. Why would you risk someone ruining it by putting his foot in his mouth or talking past her valuable message? Why would you risk a lingering moment that takes away from the momentum due to someone not being prepared or being unaware when her speech is in slated in the program?

Don't feel like you are asking too much of your speakers or your performers. You have asked or will ask those in attendance to place a value on what they have witnessed. Make sure it is worth the top dollar.

If you have multiple speakers and a master of ceremonies, make sure the scripts read like a great broadcast. They set you up in anticipation of what is next. One speaker supports another speaker. There is a consistent theme or message, just a few words repeated with every speaker..

The most important details are in the flow of your program. This means ensuring your message is clear and the need/impact is present in your statements and testimonies. You want people to speak between four to seven minutes. The average person speaks approximately 120–150 words a minute (slower is better). That means a good speech is about 1000 words. If it is much longer, it may be of value to include audience engagement, such as a survey or short tabletop activity.

Capture Information

Whether you are selling tickets or not, make sure you are getting people's information. Everyone who attends your event is possibly more than an attendee; they could be a long-term donor or volunteer. Your plans for after the event are twice as important as your planning of the event.

The more information you can gather, the better. However, at a minimum, gather the name and email address. This will allow you to engage them in some way after the event.

Now that you have these new people who have been introduced to your organization, how will you engage them in the next ninety days? It is important for you to reach out to everyone, especially the new people, who attends the event at least a couple of times.

There are multiple pieces of research that demonstrate donors are willing to make a second gift that occurs within one hundred days of the initial gift. Not only is there a greater chance these donors will be retained, but they also have a higher lifetime value over your average donors.

Engaging event attendees may be as simple as saying, "Thank You!" Re-share a testimony or impact of your mission that you shared that night. Invite them to be involved by touring your facility, volunteering, or making a gift. Then place them into your stewardship plan like you do every donor. This plan should have regularly planned engagement.

A Good Event is a Good Event

One of my most memorable stories as a child was when I was six or seven. My parents had several trees cut down and I was being Mr. Helpful with my little red wagon, loading up the wood my brother and father had split, and stacking it in the back yard. Before I knew it, the pile was taller than me.

Rather than stacking in a new place, I kept adding to the pile by throwing logs on top of the pile. It reached the point where when I added one more log to the top, the entire pile literally tumbled on top of me. When I came to, my father and our neighbors were removing the logs on top of me. I saw my mom holding my brother, and I started a dazed type of crying.

What does this story have to do with planning events? I often hear organizations talk about how they need to improve on the last event. If an event achieves 80 percent of its goal and shares the organization's mission, then it was a good event. That one more thing to make the event better, is often just one more thing, like that one more log to make the pile taller. Like that pile of wood, it could cause the entire event to tumble down. When an event accomplishes its goals, it is not necessary to do more than execute the event well.

Twice as Important

Take the time to celebrate and evaluate your success. In the non-profit world, getting to the event and having it occur is success. So take a moment to celebrate that. Then pull out those goals that you took time to establish and set up systems to gather data and evaluate the information. Your goals should be a stretch beyond what you "have to" accomplish. Achieving 80 percent of a goal means you were successful.

Within five days following your event, you should have a rally. At this rally, everyone that had a stake in the success of this event should be present. Here is where you review the numbers and event. Here is where you document and take action to start planning the next event (if there will be one).

At this meeting, follow this format:

1. Review the results—anything that has numbers, shout it from the roof tops what you accomplished (money, attendees, etc.)
   a. If there are pledge cards to open, open them together
2. What was the best part about the event (only positive thoughts, do not start the rabbit hole of criticism, or you will never do one of these again)
   a. Everyone shares
   b. One or two items per person
   c. One item must be unique
3. Outside feedback
   a. Call stakeholders who are not present to celebrate success (board members, speakers, etc.)
   b. Any feedback, only if you have it.
   c. Must be specific as to who said it and what it was about
   d. Comment on references to mission
4. What should we do differently
   a. Everyone shares
   b. Does not need to be unique
5. What do we need to do, and can we do immediately
   a. Any items that you can take funds from the event and purchase (replace rental expenses, signage, supplies)

b. Especially if you exceeded your goal, spend the money before it gets reallocated.

When it is easier to raise money from individuals, little is done to engage attendees after an event, and there seem to be no volunteers to make the event come together, it is worthwhile to evaluate why you do an event. If the answer is, "Because we always have," then it might be time to retire the event.

Engage Attendees

Be sure all attendees receive information about what your event accomplished. Invite them to engage your organization. That could be by participating in a survey or attending an activity. Remember, donors that are passionate about your cause are willing to make a second gift within one hundred days.

Engaging event attendees is the difference between growing your organization through contributions or constantly hunting for donors. This is why the time after an event is twice as important as the planning that leads up to the event.

⚒ TOOLBOX ⚒

Events can be overwhelming and a huge distraction. They can either grow the future of the organization or completely miss the mark. Be the one to ask the hard question: "Is this event still necessary?" Use information and not feelings to answer that question.

- Set clear, stretch goals for the event. If you do not achieve 80 percent, figure out why.
- Document everything. The more information you have, the better equipped you are to evaluate your event. Also, the more information you maintain, the better prepared you are for the next year.
- Make sure your biggest expense is covered before you sell the first ticket.
- Understand what resources are available, primarily people. Make sure the scope of the event matches the scope of the resources you have available.
- Mission, mission, mission! Tie the funds raised to your mission. Tell your story multiple times and in multiple ways. Having a good event is important, but knowing what attendees are supporting is even more important.
- Script your speakers and plan your program. Give a clear message and state a clear need.
- Get people's contact information. You can truly exceed event goals if you engage people immediately following an event and invite them to become more involved.
- Debrief. Take time to celebrate your success and evaluate the event.

- Conduct engagement post-event. This is extremely valuable. Many people are willing to give a gift within one hundred days of their last gift if asked and shown the need.

Chapter 10

The Courtship

A big-city girl too busy for love. A small-town tradesman (farmer, mechanic, carpenter) with no need for the complications of a relationship. The girl moves to a small town and runs into the tradesman (literally). At first, the tradesman confuses attraction for annoyance and seems bothered by the big-city girl. Day by day, the tradesman and girl seem to continually "run" into each other. Then the tradesman recognizes the attraction and begins to orchestrate more "run-ins." Before you know it, it is Christmas Eve, there is a soft snow falling, mistletoe . . . and a kiss. The big-city girl and the tradesman are holding each other, deeply in love. Then the camera flips to a mature individual who winks and waves approval of the relationship. Do you recognize the Hallmark channel plot line?

Whether we are talking about sales or fundraising, the metaphor of dating a prospect is a common one. While it would be nice if donor relationships were as obvious as the above plot line, it usually requires more than what is displayed in a ninety-minute made-for-TV movie.

[Insert shameless plug] There are many resources you can review at Fundraisingis.com. In Chapter 8, we discussed the importance of relationships and where that chapter was about understanding the value of relationships and their role in fundraising, this chapter is about the activities that progress donor relationships along. Thus, advancing the courtship.

Here are two important definitions to understanding the activities to further our relationships.

Cultivation is working with a prospective or current donor to build value and help him or her understand the impact of your organization.

Stewardship is working with a current, significant donor to help her understand her role in your organization and the impact of her gift. As a professional fundraiser, you should understand how this donor chooses to interact with you and the organization (notice I did not say *how you choose* to interact with the donor). Most likely, interactions involve multiple available tools.

Cultivation and stewardship are both proactive and reactive. Having opportunities for your stakeholders to interact with the organization throughout the year proactively keeps the donor engaged and invites prospective donors to learn about your organization. It is also important to have a clear response once a contribution is received, which includes an acknowledgment and, when appropriate, interaction with leadership. Activities in this chapter are the ones that fill out the plan we discussed in Chapter 4.

Start by Saying "Thank You"

The first part of any engagement with donors is acknowledging their gifts to your organization. By law, you only have to acknowledge individual gifts greater than $250. However, it is valuable to acknowledge every gift. In your letters, include information about how the organization has been impacted by their gifts. For instance: "Thanks to supporters like you, we have provided 20,000 meals to students in aftercare programs." It does not need to be specific to each donor's gift, but it clearly needs to demonstrate your mission.

If you are generating automated receipts that you print and mail, take the time to personalize this form letter by simply handwriting "Thank you" on the letter and some form of an impact statement.

If there is an automated receipt in response to online gifts, make sure you customize the receipt beyond the name, amount, and date. Almost every online platform allows some level customization. Be sure the receipt says, "Thank You" and provides an impact statement, such as "Your donation helped a young child wake up with a smile and able to learn because they have a meal today." On ones that don't allow a custom donation response, get your standard acknowledgment out immediately.

This is the start of your stewardship plan. Part of this plan is to acknowledge donors; the other part is to encourage involvement of your leadership. This example uses segmentation based on the size of the gift.

For example:

Up to $249: Standard acknowledgment, run every other week

$250–$499: Standard acknowledgment plus a handwritten note from a member of the development team

$500–$999: Standard acknowledgment plus a handwritten note from the executive director (this is in place of the development team member)

$1000–$2499: Standard acknowledgment plus a handwritten note from the executive director and another note from a member of the board.

$2500+: Standard acknowledgment plus a handwritten note from the executive director and a phone call from volunteer leadership.

Every donation is important, but you want to organically grow your contributions and ultimately fundraising is about relationships. Like they do in the Hallmark channel, turn those accidental meetings into more of a relationship with the personal touch.

The value of handwritten notes. As I get my mail each day, invariably the first piece of mail I open is the handwritten note. Often, it is the smallest, plainest piece of mail, except there is handwriting on the front. As a kid, I longed for any piece of mail with my name. In college, I longed for handwritten notes from godparents and aunts (as it usually meant some ice cream money). Today, I long for handwritten notes from longtime friends, as they usually announce significant events in their lives or just the chance to reconnect. In mailboxes full of bills and solicitations, this is truly good mail.

In a time of digital interaction, the analog approach screams for attention. It also solicits reaction as well, if not better than any flashy four-color mailing. Handwritten notes provide a unique value. They provide recognition when you do not have a budget for bonuses. To supporters, they mean more than a nameplate or a certificate. When emails are ignored, handwritten notes command attention.

In a world where people look for quick responses and try to provide emotion with images, handwriting provides all of that. It could be the deliberate nature of a stroke, the choice of a word, the added exclamation point, or an enthusiastic swoosh on a signature. Handwriting alone provides fluid emotion the digital world cannot give.

Donor Encouraged Events

Non-profit organizations have amazing programs and activities going on every day. In my initial discussions with non-profits, I learn about the programs they conduct, such as classes, graduations, and educational events. I find out about the frequency, who regularly attends, and the location. Immediately, I have a grin on my face and the person in front of me is puzzled as to what my grin means.

It means simply this: They shared about a graduation or an annual educational program or a class that the organization "just did." "Just did" is code for something that is ordinary to you, but to someone else, it is extraordinary. Think about your aunt's frozen chocolate chip cookies or your brother's steak and marinade. To them, it is just something they do, but for you, it is something you look forward to.

The next donor engagement or fundraising opportunity exists in things your organization does regularly. Donors would welcome the chance to observe or be a part of these activities. Make the most of these activities by making it a donor-encouraged event. This is not about changing the activity but adding a donor element. This could be simply adding thirty to forty-five minutes to graduation ceremony so donors get to mingle with graduates and their families around a few light refreshments. A chance for your donors to witness the impact they make and hear a "thank you" directly from those that benefit. This is in place of a ninety-minute donor reception that requires a great deal of time and effort, which the development team "just" cannot spare.

Another opportunity is to have program graduates or clients write a "thank you" note to a donor or three. Many of these individuals would welcome this chance to speak specifically to the people who supported them, whether they know them or not.

Organization calendars are littered with opportunities like these that only require an invitation and communication. For example, a school that has an art show, play, or science fair can simply add a reception for donors immediately before the event. A social service organization that packs comfort kits can turn the assembly line into a party for donors with a goal for number of packages completed.

Taking advantage of these events allows current and potential supporters to see the impact your organization has and the difference they make. This adds value to your organization, helps supporters understand the story, and maybe helps them create their own. It encourages the donor's relationship with the organization as well as individuals.

The benefits of using existing events to engage donors are limitless. One of the greatest being the partnership it forms between your development and program staff, along with limiting the effort and time commitment from your development staff and volunteers.

Creativity and Impact

In donor recognition and acknowledgment, rarely is it about sparkle and bling. Often, it is about the most humble way to show the difference a donor makes. I once worked with a major gifts officer who taught the real value of creative donor recognition.

Here is an example:

[Bob] had a relationship with our disaster volunteers so that they would call him when there was a home fire. Thanks to the disaster volunteers, he would have the opportunity to connect with the victims and often meet them at the site that was once their home. He would get their stories and walk through the rubble and collect a burnt picture frame or pieces of a charred cross, along with taking some impactful pictures of the damage that we could use in mission-focused activities.

He bagged up the embers and would attach a simple note: "To this family, your contribution made a difference."

This was one of the most powerful things we ever gave donors. I saw these embers displayed along with plaques and etched glass and there were often the most talked about items. Other innovative ideas for donor recognition include artwork from children or poems from participants. Most of the time, these items, which have no cost, are more valuable than any plaque.

Sharing notes and feedback from recipients of your services are also powerful tools to share with donors and ambassadors. These notes often include information that demonstrates the impact of your program. As long as they do not disclose the information of the client, these can build value in your program like any review or third party endorsement.

Celebrate your relationship. It is important that you treat your donor relationships like you do your other relationships (maybe even a little better). Whether it is a Facebook acquaintance or a longtime friend, you say "Happy Birthday."

On LinkedIn, we see when people get new jobs or promotions and say, "Congratulations." On occasion, often for no reason at all, we get together with people for coffee, lunch, or drinks. It is nice to catch up with donors and see what is happening in their worlds. People appreciate when we celebrate life events. If there is a new baby or grandchild, send a congratulatory card. If there is a death or illness, send a sympathy card.

When I was with one organization, I had a volunteer who suggested we send birthday cards to the volunteers. It was a great idea. She created a simple card on a letter-sized sheet of paper, folded into quarters. On her regular workday, the last week of the month, she would invite other volunteers to come in fold, sign, and address the cards for the next month. The staff and I would join in the effort, and we all became recharged from our "attitude of gratitude."

A volunteer at the same organization that helped with planning our fundraising events suggested we add our donors. She then would add birthdays to the profiles of donors she was friends with on social media. At some point, sympathy cards were added for deaths.

When this effort started, we had about a half-dozen of these cards that we sent out monthly. After a year, we had two dozen or more cards that we sent out each month. Within three months, I received regular comments about the cards when I was out in the community. This effort touched so many aspects (donor relationships, volunteer engagement, and an attitude of gratitude) and cost us little more than the required postage.

Become a resource. The organizations we work with are addressing big problems. Because they are such big problems, people are always looking for information about the problem and how it is being addressed. When your organization is making a dent in these problems—education, healthcare, homelessness, and addiction—people consider you and those involved with your organization as subject matter experts, so be that resource.

Many of our supporters are a part of civic organizations, including Rotary, Kiwanis, men's, and women's groups.

These groups are always looking for speakers. Have a prepared presentation that can be delivered in twenty-min and forty-five-min formats. When someone invites you to speak, make a big deal about it by shouting on social media and thanking them on your newsletters or other regular mass correspondence.

Provide information about your industry. Demonstrate to your supporters that you are aware of your industry beyond your organization. Locate great activities similar groups are doing in other cities. If you work on homelessness, share the article about the property management company employing homeless people in a neighboring state. If your group helps people with addiction, share the story of the church that has started a support group for families impacted by addiction.

Share educational information about your problem. Provide articles from the *Washington Post* that address the opioid epidemic and reports from SAMSHA on the suicide rates among homeless vets. When you share such information, supporters will see it in many ways. They may identify it as your focus on personal development or perhaps as ideas you are interested in for your organization or just good conversation starters for the next time you are together.

Google Alerts. When I worked in sales, a colleague taught me about Google Alerts. I mentioned this tool in Chapter 8. Here are the step-by-step instructions to establish these alerts:

1. Sign in to your Google account
2. In your browser search bar type in google.com/alerts
3. In the search bar that pops up, type key words or common search terms that you use regularly: "primary education programs," "homelessness in my state," or "addiction and recovery"
4. Then select your frequency: daily, weekly, or monthly
5. Google will set up a bot to search for these terms and deliver new search results to your inbox

You can set up an alert for your organization. I have found setting alerts for the organization to be extremely helpful. One way is simply being made aware when your organization is identified in an obituary.

I have used the articles that come as a result to provide valuable information to others, such as how challenges are being managed in other areas. There are often announcements of new funding opportunities that no one would have known about without these alerts.

Provide Tools and Invite Engagement

Social media and email management programs have changed our ability to interact and gather feedback from our constituents. In many ways, these activities can seem like a burden to manage. Having to put out a newsletter monthly or quarterly can turn into a point of great stress. Ensuring there are regular posts on your social media platforms can seem like the straw that breaks the camel's back. However, thanks to technology, these mediums can provide some extremely valuable feedback.

Here are some helpful hints that will help you as you build content for your newsletters and social media posts. Then, we discuss how you can evaluate response and engagement using the analytics in these programs to drive your future campaigns. These become resources and ways your constituents can invite others into your organization.

- *Provide testimonials in multiple forms.* On a regular basis, you gather amazing stories about the differences your organization makes in the community. Don't just keep them for when you are talking to donors. Record them, and put them on your website. Identify pull quotes and put them with a compelling picture. If you forgot to get a picture, find a stock picture that represents the story. Then create social media posts you can share. Find a permanent place for the story digitally. Share and share often. Invite your stakeholders (staff and volunteer leadership) to share it.
- *Use your Google alerts.* The articles you find of value in your alerts will be of value to the constituents. Include these articles in your newsletters. This demonstrates that your organization is aware about its industry.

- *Share the ordinary*. What you consider to be just something you do on a daily basis, others may find extraordinary. This could be related to the volunteers you have covering your front desk every day. It could be a class you have every week. Post these items and again, encourage your stakeholders to share. These posts are tools for your staff and supporters to invite others into your organization.

Now pay attention to the response to these posts and emails. The posts that get a great deal of engagements, not reach, on social media should be something you include in your newsletter. It could identify what you need to get more testimonies about. This may be a driver in your next appeal.

When you make your email blasts engaging, with short summaries and links that people can follow, pay attention. Look at the analytics from your email manager and see what links are getting clicked. This can become content for social media or you can drive your next appeal.

Is Your Communication Healthy

Make sure your donor relationships are healthy. Are you asking what they want and need? Do you understand what opportunities they are interested in? Are you only communicating with them when you are making an ask? Make sure you are forming healthy relationships with your donors.

There is no real relationship formula. We just click and friendships are formed. However, relationships tend to dwindle when it is more about one member of the relationship than the other. In the fundraising world, there are many suggestions about how to communicate, but the idea is the same across all these recommendations: provide information more than you ask for contributions. In most of these recommendations, it is to give information two or three times between every ask. This mantra is written in our communication: There is the suggestion that one uses the pronouns *you* and *your* more than *I* and *we* in your appeals.

Information can be communicated in many forms. It can be shared as a testimonial in an email blast. It can be an update in a newsletter that outlines the changes in your organization. It can be a face-to-face meeting to help a donor understand the impact of his gift. Information can be derived from a donor's involvement as a volunteer.

Healthy relationships have choices and opportunities. The opportunity to support your organization is truly an opportunity to make a difference and an impact. Working with your organization is an opportunity for friends to gather around a shared cause or to form new friendships around a cause. Your events are an opportunity for people to gather and celebrate their friendships as well as your cause.

Relationships also grow and community a healthy status when those involved welcome new people into the group. In fact, the strongest members in a group are always inviting others and encouraging others to grow the group. Yet, they are also excited when it is an intimate group of two or three and make the most of that opportunity.

In a healthy relationship, you can speak frankly and share your needs. We all like to believe we would help anyone in need. Sometimes, the help is just about listening and being present. Other times, help is connecting others (we all have had that friend that tries to play matchmaker). Sometimes, the help is about addressing a defined problem like moving, repairing, or assembling a piece of IKEA furniture. People love the chance to relive the way they helped you every time they see that piece of furniture—not only with you, but also with everyone else around.

Any relationship we have and value is complex. A healthy relationship requires give and take. Many of the suggestions here are much more about giving to our donors than about how to ask for gifts. If you think about your own relationships, we often receive more from our relationships when we give freely to them. Successful relationships often require making a gift of our time as well as our resources.

Document

Consider an intimate relationship. If it ends, you find that without noticing, you documented a great deal. From photos to shared Facebook posts and goofy cards to silly gifts, there are volumes of mementos we seem to trip over. It may become obvious why it ended. Months before it ended, the cute notes slowed. There were fewer shared social media posts—less pictures together. When you thumb through all these items, you can often track the highs and lows of the relationship.

This is no different from your donor relationships. Many donor management systems integrate with social media and email management systems. You can observe a change in a donor's interaction with the organization's social media and how often they open the emails. Then you examine how often you met with the donor and engaged them, and it often becomes obvious why they increased or decreased their giving.

When you spoke to them, was it about you and the organization or about them and the difference they make. Did you only contact them about giving opportunities, never about volunteer or engagement opportunities?

Documenting interactions with donors may seem tedious. And while that may be true, if you do it, chances are high that it will make your relationships more valuable. If you give it fifteen minutes at lunch and fifteen minutes at the end of the day, it is much more manageable. Also, you can take advantage of automated features, such as email management or using bcc: addresses that will allow your email correspondence to populate in the donor profile.

Any relationship requires effort. As development professionals, donors are the most important part of our position. However, we often find ourselves distracted by event details, reports, and marketing campaigns. Then we get in trouble for poor donor retention. I get it. Donor management is challenging. Anything worthwhile is.

Take time to celebrate the relationships developed with your donors:

- Say "Thank you"—you can never say it too often or too late
- Take advantage of current activities as donor engagement opportunities
- Highlight the impact your donors are making through their contributions
- Similar to a romantic relationship, celebrate it; demonstrate that you value it; and constantly fan the embers and keep it a warm relationship.
- Set up Google Alerts about your organization, your industry, and your best donors
- Document your relationship. It will be a wealth of information as your relationship progresses.

❖

CHAPTER 11

IT'S ABOUT A SMILE, A MOUSE, AND A COW

I definitely remember it at age thirteen more than when I was five. At thirteen, it was just my parents and I. My brother didn't come.

From the moment you drove through the entrance, you knew this place was special. Yes, even magical. When I was a new teenager, Epcot had just opened. I was allowed to miss school, and all my friends were envious that I was going to be among the first to visit Epcot. Coming into the park, the energy was contagious, there were people waiting outside to greet you with rub-on tattoos and balloons before you even entered the park.

My father loved talking to people and learning their stories. At Disney, they have always printed the place where the employees hail from on their name badges. Dad engaged a cast member, a young college student from Europe. With her smile and beautiful accent, she happily responded to my father, leaned in like it was a secret and shared that we should do the world showcase from the back in the morning because everyone started in the front .What great advice it was as the lines were nearly nonexistent, and we could easily get a drink or ice cream from any of the stands.

When I went back with my son, when he was thirteen, the magic was still there—even more so. Now they have trading cards that help people interact with areas within the Magic Kingdom, and you get to stop the famous Disney villains, including Cruella DeVille and Hades, from taking over the park. All the parks take advantage of their mobile app, Disney Play. In Epcot, through the app, you can help Agent P from "Phineus and Ferb" and activate displays in restaurants and stores. So cool! We probably talked about that experience with Agent P more than any other part of our time at Disney.

S. Truett Cathy, Walt Disney, Steve Bezos, and Steve Jobs were (and are in some cases) amazing innovators and visionaries who inspired innovation and vision in others.

They have had multiple books written about them and their organizations. Have you ever picked up one and looked for ways to apply their innovation and principles to your organization? A favorite quote of mine from entrepreneur, business consultant, and Catholic author Matthew Kelley says, "The most cost-effective form of professional development is reading five pages a day." Find a book about these innovators and start reading.

Just visiting these businesses, you can sense the uniqueness and understand why they stand out in their fields. When you walk into a Chick-fil-A, you know it is more about you being at their place of business then it is about a chicken sandwich. When you visit Disney, it is about transforming you to a place of magic. When I went with my son, I was in my forties, and I was transferred into my childhood and sensed every bit of awe that my son did.

I shop on Amazon because it is more than just convenient. Sometimes, it is like my nagging mother, who reminds me to replace or purchase again the things I need, usually just before I need them, such as printer ink or water filters. There are books I treasure and often purchase for my clients, including the Benvon books or *Nonprofit Board Service for the Genius.* Like the local restaurant that knows my name and some of my preferences on the menu, Amazon gives me a sense of home.

Apple is all about an association with innovation. Whether it is the iPhone or the iMac Pro, by owning these products, I am making the statement: "I want the best" or " I want to be among the most innovative."

These company founders have built their empires and are quite proud of their stories. In many ways, they share their stories of success, confident that many won't have the commitment to get there. For those who do, they are welcomed, helping raise the bar in their respective industries.

One truth about these visionaries is they have often failed but learned each time, finding new opportunities and improving their business models. Another truth is that many of their best practices can be applied in any industry, especially non-profit organizations.

The Touch

One tool that both Disney and Chick-fil-A has mastered is the touch. That is the ability to engage people at multiple points when people are present in their establishments. I have spent many hours working on this book and my blogs in a Chick-fil-A. While in the restaurant, I feel as taken care of as if I was visiting my favorite aunt. For the hour or so that I sit and type, people have picked up my tray, refilled my drink, and brought me a couple of mints. That is after I have paid my ticket and eaten my food. Prior to getting my food, they greeted me at the door, took my order, and delivered my order to the table. If you have been in a Chick-fil-A drive-through lately, they rarely use a faceless voice box but have cashiers working the drive-through line, taking orders. Another takes my money or provides me with a receipt. Finally, I receive my food from a third worker.

At Disney, they either have greeters standing in the streets inside the park, or the people in the retail establishments are there in the down times. Cast members are everywhere, ready to help. Disney's commitment to ensuring families' outstanding experiences was explained at the Disney Leadership Institute. When you have one kid crying and one kid tugging, you do not want to have to hunt for assistance or be directed somewhere else for assistance. You want the help and access when you need it.

My favorite grocery store growing up was Ukrop's. A local family owned business. Many of my friends got their first jobs as baggers at Ukrop's. They shared that a rule there was that if a customer was looking for an item, they did not give the isle number. They walked them to the item and did not leave them until they touched it or picked it up.

In a world of artificial intelligence (AI) and digital interaction, people want a quick response, but they also want a personal response. AI can only respond to the questions asked, not necessarily recognize the need or understand the situation as a person can. Many of our mail management systems have amazing schedulers and systems that help us engage our donors after their first gift. Do not forget that much more can occur in an initial phone call, such as understanding how they became connected to our organization, which is extremely valuable and will not occur because of a two-week-later email that shares an impactful story.

Presentation is Everything

My mother always said, "Presentation is everything." This is extremely true at Disney. One major rule they have is: "Don't let backstage come onstage." More than just letting patrons see where the magic happens, it is about making sure that you always put your best foot forward and invite others to be a part of the magic. In a documentary about the early days of Disneyland, Walt was walking through the park and noticed a trail being cut through the grass. Immediately, he had the landscaping team install a brick-laid path. He used the patrons' habits to help determine Disneyland's layout.

In the Disney Leadership Institute, we learned there is less than twenty feet between trash receptacles. That is a lot of trash receptacles. The reason is because decision-makers continued to add trash receptacles until they stopped finding trash on the ground. Why? A trash receptacle is cheaper, and people will dispose of their trash if you give them the opportunity.

At Amazon, the website layout is one of the ugliest I have ever witnessed. However, did you know, in essence, each Amazon customer has its own custom website? A great deal of what I see when I log into Amazon is based my experience each time I visit. It's like when I traveled to West Virginia to visit my favorite aunt, and she had Pringles and Hi-C and many other of my favorites, even though her children had long ago moved out of the house. She, like Amazon, made me feel special in her home.

People are Your Greatest Asset

S. Truett Cathy is very transparent about the value he places on his people, from the operating agreement to the expectations he places on the people Chick-fil-A hires. He openly discusses the importance of faith and self-motivation. Throughout the books he wrote, he passionately discusses how he invests in young people. One of his books is literally called *It is Better to Build Boys Than Mend Men*.

In a similar way, Disney is straightforward about their expectations, well before they hire you. At the Disney Leadership Institute, they shared how before applicants turn in their applications, they must watch a video about the non-negotiables. These are attitudes and characteristics that are accepted and not accepted by cast members. It requires that all tattoos are covered; there is a limit on visible piercings; foul language is prohibited; and tardiness is not acceptable. After the video, an applicant can choose to put in their application or exit the building.

Amazon pays their line workers well because of the expectations they place on them. All of these organizations realize the importance and value of the people in their employ. They know that they make a difference with the experience of their patrons.

All of these organizations have extensive training and mentoring programs. Disney and Chick-fil-A invest in the work environment. They both ask for feedback from the public about their cast members and make big deals over both the good and the bad feedback. In multiple books about Disney, there are chapters about how "little wows" add up. In Chapter 7, I wrote about the "starfish" principle—the story of a young boy throwing starfish back into the ocean as he and an old man walk a beach filled with starfish and explains to the old man, "To that one I made a difference."

In many situations, our employees can demonstrate greatness if just empowered to do so. When I worked for Enterprise, everything from our beginning titles to our daily operations spoke to this. When you join the Enterprise team, you are a management trainee. The title itself communicates they are preparing you to move into a larger role. If there was a customer issue, you were encouraged and empowered to remedy it. Everyone could use the customer satisfaction account. It did not require manager approval. It was part of empowering people and expecting the best.

Innovation Can Be Simple

When we are talking about innovation, we often think about Macintosh and its first WYSIWYG (what you see is what you get) platform or Apple's iPhone with its touchscreen keyboard and app technology. Most innovation is not that complicated, nor requires a great deal of advanced technology. When I first witnessed the young people taking orders from the drive-through line at Chick-fil-A, all they were doing were calling in the orders through their headsets from the line. There were no tablets or mobile pay systems.

At the Disney Leadership Institute, they shared how a parking lot attendant started shading in a map of the parking lot each quarter hour in the morning. That way, when tired families came out of the park and could not remember where they parked, the attendant just need to find out when they arrived and could take them close.

When I worked for Enterprise, I suggested that instead of handing out bound training manuals each time we got promoted, they give us a binder at the start. I figured it would cut down on lost handouts since we often needed them for our next required training. A binder was something we could easily add more to and could include loose-leaf paper for notes. Then as we entered management, we had a resource book as we participated in training new employees. I received a reward and a handwritten note from the regional HR manager for that idea.

The truth is most of the innovations these organizations and their founders' biographies talk about are low-cost or no-cost concepts. In fact, they often add value (revenue opportunity) or save money. For instance, the all-in-one design of the original Mac saved production costs. And the additional trashcans at Disney (so you don't go more than twenty feet without passing one) saved them money. My binder idea saved money and helped managers become better trainers.

Be Unique

Uniqueness is available in many forms. Being unique can be using a simple statement, such as, "My pleasure" or placing an "i" in front of any product name—iPhone. More importantly, it can be in the way you treat your constituents. Charity: Water has found uniqueness by saying that 100 percent of every gift goes toward their mission. They do this by reaching out to people with the capacity to cover their overhead expenses. It's not a strategy everyone can use, but it is unique.

I recently received my first video "Thank You." It was someone videotaping from her phone and showed me in moving images the impact of my small gift. It was short, simple, unique, and innovative.

When I think about the reward I received for my binder idea, I could not tell you the amount or item, but I can tell you about Gretchen's note. I still have it! That was unique to me, as a twenty-something in my first job.

Most non-profit organizations do not have the footprint of Chick-fil-A, Disney, Apple, or Charity: Water. Being unique is not about our brand as much as it is about being unique to our donors. Every day, there are new non-profits seeking a donor's dollar. How will you stand out among the rest?

Application

Even though these are mostly retail industries, there are many ideas we can learn and apply to the non-profit industry. If you brainstorm and think about how you interact with donors, there are multiple opportunities.

Think about how you interact with donors and create touch points with them. Are you involving multiple people in your donor engagement? Think about the relationships discussed in Chapter 8. Concepts, such as the relationship triangle and the story about how much stronger a bundle of sticks are than a single twig, can be helpful.

Consider your events. How do you welcome people to your event? Are you making contact with people from the moment they enter the building? How do you engage them throughout the event?

While being unique, have you examined your recognition or the way you thank your donors. Could you be unique in the way you explain the difference or impact your donors make? Maybe it is in providing a unique name for the giving society or in explaining the impact. It could be in the gift that you give to donors.

Do you provide innovation in how you deliver your services? It could be a unique prayer or pledge your volunteers or clients make. It could be in the process that you follow in evaluating clients. All of these are a part of your story and can add value to why donors choose to support you.

Are the expectations clear to your employees? How have you built your "culture of philanthropy" between the program and development staff? Is there a fundraising expectation when someone joins the organization? Take time to recognize the value of internal relationships with handwritten notes or special gifts.

Many of the books mentioned in this chapter are located at pbjmarcomm.net/resources.

✗ TOOLBOX ✗

- Read about other industry leaders
- Identify the "uniqueness" of your organization
- Engage and listen to your constituents (idea boxes, donor surveys)

CHAPTER 12

EVENTUALLY YOU HAVE TO

There he was. He had thought about this moment for a while now. Even rehearsed it a few times, anticipating different responses. It was time, but he still felt unprepared. At least it wasn't his first time, and previously, it had gone pretty well . . .

Still, his heart was racing. His palms were clammy. There was unease in the stomach.

We are either describing a teenage boy getting ready to ask out someone he has been noticing for weeks, or we are talking about a professional fundraiser getting ready to make his first five-figure ask. Both have similar symptoms. A lack of self-confidence countered with a personal pep talk. A sense of urgency combined with a desire to make a difference and be unique (but are you really?).

There has to be an "ask." A request for money. A request to fund a valuable need. What we, as professional fundraisers, see as an awkward conversation. As my friend, Phil Perdue, wrote in his book, *May I Cultivate You?*, "People are a little crazy. And we are a little crazy for trying to get money from them."

I am sure when I sit in front of donors that I appear crazy. Uncomfortably, I sit in front of them, and in some nuanced way proceed to ask them for a significant gift. They are always extremely gracious and accommodating; I can only imagine the conversations they have with their peers or family afterward about my visit. When it replays in my mind, it is always much more awkward and seems like a "Saturday Night Live" skit. In my head, I am sweating buckets or changing five shades of a pale green, and I'm always fidgety, much like a toddler having to pee. Regardless of how long I have been doing this, whether we are talking about closing a major deal or making a major ask my nightmares could only make sense of via the show "Ally McBeal," it's difficult. (Ally McBeal was a hit show in the 1990s, which I'm using to date myself.)

The principle of this book is there is a great deal to fundraising and then there is asking for money. I am not aware of an organization that has someone knocking down its door to give it its operating budget for the year. That is why we have jobs—someone needs to be asking for support. In a perfect world, one earns the right to ask for money. There is a significant amount of groundwork put in place through stewardship and cultivation. Unfortunately, the groundwork is often skipped, and then there is a need for a fundraiser to lean on a relationship that is not his own.

People Act Emotionally and Justify Logically

In sales, it's called finding the pain. In philanthropy, it's identifying the problem. In sales and philanthropy both, it's about the solution you proffer. In philanthropy, we use images of adorable or bedraggled kids in need or images of poverty and disaster to drive donors' emotion. Unlike sales, though, we do not hold the solution, our donors do. We give donors the opportunity to make a difference for one starfish

One of the most powerful things I learned in my career was that people act emotionally and justify logically. Think about the candy at the register and how so much of it is chocolate. How many different ways do we justify buying that bag of M&Ms?

We ask donors to give of their affinity and offer options based on different ways they can make an impact. Many have said that fundraising is storytelling. Our storytelling is compelling and is designed to touch the heart. They are amazing stories of transformation. We drive emotion and connect with our donors desire to make a difference when we start pulling on those heartstrings. We can hardly get through the story of that family that was helped without starting to get emotional. There is much more about this in Chapter 7.

It Can't Be Nuanced

While working with clients, I have heard, "She is aware of our need." How? Has she been a project manager who can estimate the costs in her head? Does she have her own advisory board that secretly researches every non-profit project that is presented?

I am very impressed by our colleagues in higher education when it comes to major gift requests; they put it in the form of a proposal. Presenting a formal explanation of the project as a clear and concise ask to include: its cost, timeline, and predicted outcomes.

Giving societies are an amazing tool and invite people to make a significant impact for just "a few dollars a day." Most giving societies request a regular gift and/or some long-term pledge. The different levels explain a donor's long-term impact to motivate him or her to follow-through on the commitment. Most people don't realize that $1000 is less than $85/month. When they do, they are excited about the impact they *can* make. Unfortunately, like Christmas decorations, giving societies are mostly brought out for a single event rather than being used by leadership as an opening discussion with donors. All your tools need to be "used" regularly.

However you ask, it needs to be specific and mission-focused. Understand that daily operations are still mission-focused. You can't run your organization without people, facilities, or essentials like transportation.

If It Were Easy, Everyone Would Do It

Let's be honest, asking for money is not easy. In some ways, it's unnatural to ask people to give without getting anything tangible in return. At least that is what we think and society suggests.

Many people are embracing this concept by asking people to give to their favorite causes rather than purchase a birthday or anniversary gift. Charity: Water has an amazing story about Rachel, a nine year old, who raised $220 through her birthday fundraiser (when she wanted to raise $300). Before she had a chance to do it again, she was killed in a car accident. Her story inspired others and her family ended up raising $1.2 million dollars through birthday fundraisers.

Most people are honored that you asked them to be included and will honestly respond. If they can't or it is something they do not want to support, they will respond accordingly. In most cases, we are asking people to give from their excess. Not the funds they need to put food on the table or roofs over their heads. Very few will give when they cannot afford, especially if you respect any gift or action (such as time or prayers). When they can give financially, if it something they are passionate about, they will seek the opportunity again.

Even with all the experience and contrasting information, fundraisers can struggle to make the appointment to make an "ask." They even struggle with setting that first meeting, even though there will be no discussion of money. "Dissonance" is the act off doing anything and everything other than what needs to be done.

Talking with donors and strengthening relationships is our job. As much as we try to bring people into our environment, major gifts are often a result of going out and stepping into the donor's environment. Self-help gurus have written volumes on how you should do the most painful, most difficult, the most challenging of activities first. That way you tend to accomplish a lot more. Is talking to donors painful, difficult, or challenging? Most often not. It is the asking for money that many people consider being painful, challenging, and difficult.

Start by Asking More

Having the knowledge that asking for money is hard, take time to ask about the donor and his or her interest in your organization. The ability to question is a skill. To inquire graciously through probative questions is a unique skill. Like any important skill, it is necessary to practice and develop that skill. Answering and asking questions is also necessary to the start of any relationship.

Earlier in this book, I mentioned interviews for jobs; they are filled with questions. The strongest candidates are the ones prepared with questions of their own. Consider a first date, it is a volley of questions in conversation to consider if there is mutual interest for a second date. So why do we equip our fundraisers with a bevy of statistics and a laundry lists of needs when we send them to meet with donors (especially when it is their first meeting with said donor)?

As fundraisers, we could learn something from those in the "program" side of our organizations. They are quite adept at learning about and understanding the need for our organization's services. Whether it is case managers conducting triage to prioritize a client's needs or an educator interacting with a child to assess their skills-readiness, the members of our team that deliver our services, understand that it takes relationship and trust to often get individuals to use the services we offer, despite their individual needs. The same trust is necessary when we are identifying investors in our organization.

In addition, it takes understanding the difference between open-ended and closed-ended questions. There is extraordinary value in using "continuing questions," such as "really?" or "You don't say?" Most importantly, having these relationship building conversations takes practice. No great player walks onto a court and is instantly a champion without practice, nor is a speaker admired because they are unscripted or unrehearsed.

Another requirement is to develop a routine. Athletes work on routines and plays, which they use over and over regardless of the situation. To get comfortable, we need our own routines so we become comfortable interacting with donors. A basketball player takes hundreds of foul shots before they take one in a game. To that extent, create a list of starter questions and topics that you want to focus on. Then, engage those people in the program side or colleagues and role-play those starter questions.

Keep It About the Donor

When you make an "ask," make sure you keep the focus on the donor. The conversation is not about all the things your organization can do as a result of a certain gift. It is about the impact the donor makes as a result of the gift.

When I was in sales leadership, I would explain when the need for the sale is more important than the benefit to the customer, it would cost you the sale. The same is true for garnering a contribution. If getting a donation is more important than connecting with the donor and the difference the donor will make, it will cost you the contribution. We have all heard the pleas that shout, "If we don't get $10,000, we will have to close the doors." They don't work. It makes it about the organization and not the donors or the mission itself.

Your organization may be one of the most fiscally responsible ones out there. It may only cost you pennies on the dollar to operate your organization. But the point of your meeting is not about the operations; it is about the mission. Regardless of the percentage of every donation that covers your overhead, the value one needs to communicate is that every donation helps you to accomplish your mission. That includes the overhead. It would be great if people could afford to donate their time and real estate moguls could donate property and stores could donate supplies, and so on and so forth, but they can't. A donation to you does more than just your mission; there is also impact to the local economy. Donors make a difference.

Prepare to Cascade

Sometimes, when you have prepared the perfect proposal or think you understand the donor and have connected the "ask" with the impact, it's just not as perfect as you thought. Have some alternatives ready. These options are not necessarily specific to this donor but are specific to the organization.

This is called cascading. When the initial proposal does not work, you have a toolbox of standard options that allows you to restart the relationship. One option may be a standard "ask," such as a pledge form or giving society you have prepared with a story and impact for different giving levels. This is part of the reason I believe in giving societies. These societies are an amazing tool for your team. Not only do they allow the organization to plan, but they also are a defined way of engagement.

Ask for many small gifts rather than one large gift. We talked about a giving society, but giving society levels may not fit everyone, so offer flexibility with alternate amounts and different pledge periods. Depending on the scale of the gift, could you ask the donor to make a monthly contribution that would add up to the amount you seek. If significant, the opportunity could be for a multi-year pledge. By offering options like these, you place the donor in control, allowing everyone to think creatively and giving the donor a way to still make an impact.

Another option could be a standard engagement opportunity. This could be a point of entry tour or a quarterly work project. There are multitudes of research studies that demonstrate those who volunteer are more likely to contribute. Sometimes a "no" or a "not now" is really a sign that the donor wants to KNOW more about your organization. Education and volunteering offer individuals a unique snapshot into your organization, its mission, and the culture.

Some Will, Some Won't

Making an "Ask" is not a guarantee for receiving a gift. In some cases, making an "ask" is not a guarantee for a gift . . . yet. The importance of these two statements is about understanding what a donor means when they say "no."

It would be helpful if every response was a clear response, such as YES or NO. However, it is not always that clear. A NO could be a straight up "No, I am not interested in making a donation to your organization!" (That is the easy one.) A no could be a "not at this time." This is where the interpretation begins and good inquiry helps to decide how to progress with this donor. Is this a nice way of saying there is no interest in supporting your organization or is the donor indicating, "This is not an opportune time for me?" You have to ask for clarity. If someone is truly interested in your organization, there will be an invitation to return to the conversation or an explanation of the limiting factor (they need cash for another project).

The other type of no is a contribution, but a contribution that is far from the expected amount. Again, there is a level of interpretation. This could be because you completely missed the capacity of this particular donor, or the donor wants you to go away, or the donor wants to see what you do with this gift.

Fundraising and major gifts is a numbers game. The more you ask, the more you receive, and the better the revenue.

The more you engage donors (fundraising), the better you can predict the likelihood of a gift and gift amount. There are two things to focus on. First, on average, organizations lose 80 percent of donors after the first gift. Focusing on the first-time donors (people who have already said they are interested in giving) opens a great deal of revenue opportunity. Next, always remember there are plenty of donors. Just like Mom said, "There are plenty of fish in the sea" when it came to dating, be looking out beyond your doors to fish.

It is OK to bless and release donors. If the response is "no", then you should have some permissions you can ask. You make ask permission to send updates on activities. You may ask permission to visit them again in six months. You may ask permission to invite them to you signature event. If the response to these requests is indifferent or lacking interest, it is OK to ask permission to wait until they contact you. Thus, taking them out of your portfolio and your cycle of follow-ups. Be sure to document your conversation to save others from the situation. This is blessing and releasing donors.

Make Sure You Have the Right Person

It is important that the people you are speaking with are truly the decision-makers. One of the most valuable questions to ask them is how they choose the organizations donors consider supporting. If it is a family you're approaching, who is part of the decision? I once heard of a family that made a multi-generational gift during the holidays. The decision was made during Thanksgiving dinner, and the decision was often influenced by the experiences of the newest generation.

In many husband and wife teams, research demonstrates that wives often drive the decisions more than husbands. When talking to funders, ask for proposals that have been funded in the past and see who is on the decision-making team that you can meet with.

Good inquiry skills will help you to identify the most influential individuals in securing a major gift.

Asking Becomes Natural

When you take time to learn many of the suggestions in this book, making an "ask" becomes natural. In many cases, it comes as a response to donors' questions of "How can I help?" One colleague called it reaching a mutual agreement.

Fundraising is fun, especially when you accept that it is not about asking for money. When you take the time to get to know your donors and their motivations, it is fun. Communicating with donors about the differences they make is motivating. Inviting and encouraging donors to be a part of your programs and witness their impact is heartwarming. When donors consider themselves partners in your success, they want to do their parts. Doing all the little things, which add up to be a lot, allows the "ask" to become a natural part of conversation.

I Hope This Helped

There are many ways to ask for money: online, direct mail, events, in person. To achieve the greatest success, it takes a good deal more than just making an "ask." Whether it's in the form of a letter, email blast, or face-to-face conversation, the groundwork needs to be laid. This book covered many aspects of that groundwork and is designed so that you can review each section independently.

- Building a foundation within your organization
- Developing a plan
- Having the right equipment
- Telling a great story
- Owning relationships
- Focusing on stewardship and cultivation
- Learning from others.

This book is one of many great books on fundraising. Non-profits are businesses, and the development team is the front-line sales team. In all honesty, fundraisers are the best sales people in the market. This is for one primary reason: They are passionate about and believe in the mission of the organization. This single characteristic helps them stand out. Where typical salespeople may believe in their products, the motivation is the nearly always the commission. The close is attached to a personal incentive, such as a car or vacation. For the professional fundraiser, the close is connected to the wellbeing of the community—meals provided, lifesaving research, homes restored, or a dozen other worthy causes. Think about it; you're not asking for yourself, you are asking to make the world a better place for many.

As a professional with a non-profit, THANK YOU for the difference you make.

⚒ TOOLBOX ⚒

- Know your story – include the impact and the difference a donor can make
- Be clear in what you are asking for
- Develop a list of questions to use with donors
- Practice asking with colleagues or other staff members
- Be prepared for common objections
- Focus on the donor and the difference they make
- Be prepared for no
- The more you practice, the more you do, the easier it becomes

⚒

CRISIS FUNDRAISING

W hile writing *Fundraising Is: Everyone Done Before Asking For Money*, COVID-19 hit the world. There is no story I could tell—fiction or true—that would compare with the numerous real-life stories that emerged during the COVID-19 outbreak. The impact on the market, the drastic change in, the cancellation of events, and the drive to promote social distancing all seemed like something that only happens in movie plots.

The pandemic crisis has impacted so much. However, this bonus chapter is about how to conduct your planning during any crisis. Where the COVID-19 crisis is clearly the fringe of what anyone could imagine, there are some hard and fast rules that apply to any crisis. Whether we are talking about hurricanes, flu outbreaks, financial crises, or an organizational crisis (your building caught on fire), there is a "formula" for kicking your fundraising into high gear.

The most important thing to remember is that it's about your mission, not about the money. Donors and stakeholders support you because of the mission you carry out, and also because you are a successful and worthwhile business. You fill in the cracks.

Two Plans

It begins with having a plan . . . actually two plans. The first plan is your communications plan for while the crisis is active. This plan is often reactionary and develops daily. Communication is critical and should be amped up during the crisis. It is important that your message is clear as to what your organization is in need of and the impact that your organization is making during the crisis.

How is the organization telling its story during a crisis? A crisis requires your organization (and you) to be nimble and agile and ready to adapt and overcome. The organization may need to reschedule an event or launch an unplanned campaign to support your efforts. Maybe, your organization will have to address programs, processes, and protocols to conduct business. Hopefully, this is not your first time facing such a situation. If you have experience, it was well documented, and you have a resource library to pull from, you will likely prevail. If you do not have a library, this is the opportunity to build a library.

This library and the storytelling opportunities are what drive the second plan. How and what the organization is doing during this time of crisis is the content of your second plan. The second plan is all about letting your constituency know how the organization is continuing to serve and remain relevant during the crisis. If it is a natural disaster, then is your organization providing water, resources, and shelter as people recover? If it is a financial crisis, how is the organization adapting and helping the public maintain a certain "quality of life."

Regardless if you are working on the initial plan or your post-crisis plan, here are some things that need to be part of your plan. These items can either be sections in your plans or conversation starters as the strategy is developed.

Communicate, Communicate, Communicate

Communication is key. Since your mission is valuable, everything that you do has value, so be sharing everything in every format possible (social media, website, newsletters). Your mission is about people and pictures of people which tell stories. As often as possible, share pictures, share stories, and consequently, share value.

Develop a plan for all your venues. Know how you will communicate, how often you will communicate, and what you will communicate. During a crisis, communication needs to increase in every way: more emails, more social media posts, and more phone calls.

Remain relevant. During COVID-19, many groups took advantage of the virtual world and the need for content. Some organizations created instructional videos that people could use to conduct activities at home and occupy their time. Some showcased their leaders speaking to those stuck at home, saying they are not alone and announcing a change in services. If you work with seniors, help them fill their medicines and get groceries. If you work with children, do virtual reading. If you help out in disasters, publish videos about creating a disaster preparedness kit for your kids or for your families. The great thing about all this is that it's content that you can use later and across multiple platforms.

Evaluate it. Look at your social media numbers. Look at changes in your traffic to your website. Review your email tracking. If there is a social media post that is getting a great deal of engagement, can you cross-post onto your website or in an email.

Communicate Intimately

As easy as mass communication is through mass emails or social media posts, this is a time to communicate with donors one-on-one. You can communicate by doing individual emails, texts messages, and phone calls. When feasible, conduct in-person visits.

If you have never communicated this way, expect suspicion. During times of regional, national, or international crises, donors get bombarded with requests by many worthy causes. Donors are seeking authentic communication, so provide it following these rules:

Be positive. This is a challenging time. It is a challenging time for donors as well as your organization. Share empathy, but be positive. Again that your organization offers value and remains important. If there is a great story that has been shared on social media, reference that.

Begin with a thank you. The people you are reaching out to already have some sort of relationship with you and have given in the past. Say, "Thank You." Be specific about how their support has benefited your organization in the past. If you can speak to a specific program, provide information on that.

Speak to your mission. Tell people your elevator speech to remind them what your mission is. Be sure to include the individual stories that exemplify your mission. If you can speak to the long-term impact of your mission by sharing an update of someone you have worked with, that is a bonus.

Other conversation starters. Verify information—check the name, address, phone number, and email. Get the information that is missing, especially emails.

Create new opportunities. Most databases have fields for birthdays and/or anniversaries. This is a future opportunity to engage donors. Everyone loves a birthday card. All you need to do is send them out at the start of the month.

Survey the donors. Ask them how they feel about your current communication. What is the best communication they have received? What is there favorite program? Take the time to listen.

Know Your Data

Speak to where you are today and what it will take to get you to the next step. You are making these calls because something has occurred, and there is a revenue shortage (an event was canceled, significant damage occurred, and revenue was removed). Most of us do not have a piggy bank in a donor that can cover the short fall.

Know what will be impacted and what the specific costs associated with the individual programs will be. Be prepared to speak to what you believe a specific donor will be able to assist with.

For example, if you have a $100,000 impact and do not have one donor you believe can replace that impact, then you need to break that impact down.

- $10,000 for a reading program
- $1000 will cover this reading program for twenty children for the next thirty days

- $25,000 for a feeding program
- $500 will cover meals for twenty children for one week.
- *Operational costs. You need to operate, and there are people that want to fund this so you can continue the good work you are doing*
- $5000 will cover our rent/mortgage for the next month.

Work Your Data

This is when you donor management system comes to value. Identify different reports you can work. Here are some ideas:

- Lapsed donors—thank them for previous support, explain how important their support is now
- Top donors—explain the impact of their contributions in the past, ask for advice (get money)
- Outstanding pledges—if you have a giving society, ask for an "advance on the pledge." Make sure you address any automatic payments
- Prospective donors—set up a special giving page and prepare a solid message and invite those "prospects" to give, or use ambassadors to share the page and invite other donors.

Be Open to All Help

Remember the old cliché: If you want money, ask for advice. If you want advice, ask for money. This cliché is very true. So be willing to listen to advice. When given, follow-up and share what you did or did not do with the advice. If people offer to write a check, be prepared with what level you want them to give. That is why it is important to know the numbers.

Forget Egos

This is not a time to claim ownership of specific donors or limit who can be involved. This is a time to focus on the right person, right time, and right ask. This is a crisis, and all hands are on deck. If you have others who feel they can help, take the time to educate, prep, and empower them.

Under-Promise/Over-Deliver

Whatever you say you will do in your conversations with donors at this time, do more. If you promise a report by Friday, get it to them on Thursday. If you promise one picture of a program, provide two. Whatever you do, make that donor believe they are the most important and most valuable person in the world. If you only do handwritten notes at $500, start doing them at $250. A crisis will pass, but it takes some extra effort to succeed in this time.

Be Innovative and Creative

During COVID-19 and at other times, people were isolated. If you want to get in with an elderly donor, offer to pick up groceries for them. If you have children's artwork setting around, use it as part of your thank you/solicitation.

If you have extra trinkets from a previous event, send them out in some unique way with a special message, especially if you have something, such as hand sanitizer during COVID-19!

Document, Document, Document

Every crisis is unique, but what is needed is not. The available resources are often the same. Some things will be done really well and should be considered the next time you have a crisis (though, no guarantee it will work next time). Some things will crash and burn yet should still be considered for the next crisis (that activity may be more appropriate). It is important to record why something succeeded or failed.

Record timelines and activities. Some things would have gone better if they had been instituted earlier. Part of the challenge for many organizations is starting from scratch at each crisis. Instead, create a library or a folder that will help you the next time your organization steps into a crisis.

Don't forget about the brainstorms that are conducted, but the ideas are never used. Often, ideas are feasible, but the crisis ends before they can be executed. Include them in your library.

This does not have to be formal documentation. It can be a handwritten note. It can be a blown-up picture of a whiteboard. It can be notes on the outside of the folder. The only formal documentation should be any strategy, plan, or activity that was executed (review the post-event debrief in Chapter 9). The value of this is to create a starting point for the next crisis. Make this a folder that is reviewed with others at the start of the next crisis to begin the brainstorming and prevent reinventing solutions to create calm and confidence.

About the Author

 Patrick Belcher instructs local non-profit organizations on how to consistently raise money. His passion lies with guiding charities in developing long-term strategies to gather resources that help them achieve their missions.

Patrick discovered how his sales background applied to fundraising while working for the American Red Cross where he exceeded fundraising goals. As a consultant, he has worked with local affiliates of national groups, such as Adult & Teen Challenge. He has also worked with local addiction and recovery centers, organizations that support the arts, local private schools, and other groups focused on education.

Learn more about the strategies Patrick uses with his non-profits on his blog at Pbjmarcomm.net.

Glossary

Cultivation: The activities done to develop a relationship with a prospective contributor, or to move a current donor to a significantly higher contribution.

Culture of Philanthropy: The belief that everyone in the organization has a role in fundraising because fundraising is not asking for money. It could be collecting stories about the organization impact. It could be connecting prospective donors with leadership. It could be building awareness in the community.

Donor Base: The evaluated list of donors that an organization has to work with for its funding needs.

Engagement: Stepped process of turning potential donors into donors.

Friendraising: A social activity that is focused on strengthening relationships or using existing relationships to identify new relationships. May include a soft solicitation, but the focus is to create relationships and build awareness of the organization.

Hard Solicitation: A direct asks for support through an event or activity. Support focused on a specific program or campaign. Usually has a published goal.

MacGyver: Someone who can fix a problem with minimal resources.

Operational Costs: The line items in your budget that is necessary for your organization to operate. That could be rent/ mortgage for a facility, certain administrative personnel, or other expenses that cannot be associated with program or mission delivery.

Segmentation: Separating your donor lists into targeted populations to solicit based organization needs and donor motivation.

Soft Solicitation: An opportunity to support the organization as the part of another activity, such as a donate button as part of a newsletter or a donation box at a public event.

Starfish Principle: The concept that to one person, one family, one community you are making a difference. It is not about the large statistics but the singular impact and how that can be transferred to any individual.

The Statistic of One: Focusing on the mission of the organization through an individual's story. This allows the individual listening to transfer the situation to a situation they are familiar with.

Stewardship: The activities done to maintain a relationship with a current contributor to the organization.

Transference: The ability for an individual contributor to connect with the individual(s) represented in a story because they share characteristics with someone the donor is familiar with.

Endnotes

Chapter 1

Barnard, Ed. "Climbing Mount Rainier – Mental and Emotional Preparation." *Visit Rainier*, accessed 24 Aug 2020, https://visitrainier.com/climbing-mount-rainier/.

IMDb. "MacGyver" (TV Series, 1985–1992), https://www.imdb.com/title/tt0088559/.

Jones, Roy and Andrew Olsen. *Rainmaking: The Fundraiser's Guide to Landing Big Gifts.* CreateSpace, 2013.

Shepherd, R. Daniel. "Zen and the Art of Moves Management." Accessed 24 Aug 2020, https://thefrontlinefundraiser.com/wp-content/uploads/2018/04/Zen.Moves-Whitepaper.pdf.

Sargeant, Adrian, Amy Eisenstein, and Rita Kottasz. "Major Gift Fundraising: Unlocking the Potential for your

Nonprofit," *Mastering Major Gifts.* Accessed 24 Aug 2020, https://masteringmajorgifts.com/report/.

Chapter 2

Renaissance Man. DVD. Directed by Penny Marshall. Detroit: Cinergi Pictures Entertainment, Parkway Productions, and Touchstone Pictures, 1994.

Chapter 3

Sargeant, Adrian, Eisenstein, Amy, and Rita Kottasz. "Major Gift Fundraising: Unlocking the Potential for your Nonprofit," *Mastering Major Gifts.* Accessed 24 Aug 2020, https://masteringmajorgifts.com/report/.

Pollock, Sara. "7 Turnover Statistics You Can't Unlearn (Number 5 is the Worst)." *Clear Company.* 18 March 2020, Accessed 25 Aug 2020. https://blog. clearcompany.com/7-turnover-statistics-you-cant-unlearn-number-5-is-the-worst.

Chapter 4

Heath, Dan. *Upstream: The Quest To Solve Problems Before They Happen.* New York: Avid Reader Press/Simon & Schuster, 2020.

Chapter 7

Toy Story, DVD. Directed by John Lasseter. Los Angeles: Pixar Animation Studios, 1995.

Grisham, John. *A Time to Kill.* New York: Dell, 2009.

Risk, Mary. "The Pixar Storytelling Formula: An Inside Look." *Studiobinder.* 24 April, 2017, Accessed 25 Aug 2020. https://www.studiobinder.com/blog/the-pixar-storytelling-formula-an-inside-look/?pixar-youtube.

Chapter 8

Yoruk, Baris K. "Do charitable solicitations matter? A Comparative Analysis of Fundraising Methods." SUNY-Albany, Department of Economics, 12 Sept 2010, Accessed 25 Aug 2020. https://www.albany.edu/economics/research/workingp/2010/Fund_methods.pdf.

Chapter 9

Independent Sector. "Independent Sector Releases New Value of Volunteer Time of $25.43 Per Hour." 11 April 2019, Accessed 15 August 2020. https://independentsector.org/news-post/new-value-volunteer-time-2019/

Chapter 11

Schaefer, Susan and Bob Wittig. *Nonprofit Board Service for the GENIUS.* For the GENIUS Press, 2015.

Chapter 12

Perdue, Philip. *May I Cultivate You?*. Petar Publishing, 2017.

IMDb. "Ally McBeal" (TV Series, 1997–2002), https://www.imdb.com/title/tt0118254/.

Charity: Water. https://archive.charitywater.org/rachels-gift/.

A free ebook edition
is available with the
purchase of this book.

Print & Digital Together Forever.

Snap a photo

Free ebook

Read anywhere